Catch 'em, Hook 'em, and Cook 'em

Catch'em, Hook'em, and Cook'em

§ TWO VOLUMES IN ONE §

by Bunny Day

Drawings by Grambs Miller

GRAMERCY PUBLISHING COMPANY
NEW YORK

This edition is published by Gramercy Publishing Company, a division of Crown Publishers, Inc., by arrangement with Doubleday & Company, Inc.
   b c d e f g h
1980 PRINTING

Manufactured in the United States of America

Library of Congress Cataloging in Publication Data

Day, Eleanor F
   Catch 'em, hook 'em, and cook 'em.

   Originally published in 2 v. by Doubleday, Garden City, N.Y., the 1st published in 1961 under title Catch 'em and cook 'em; the 2d published in 1962 under title Hook 'em and cook 'em.
   Includes index.
   1. Cookery (Shellfish) 2. Cookery (Fish) 3. Fishing. I. Title.
TX753.D3 1980   641.3'9   79-27626
ISBN 0-517-31436-3

Catch'em
and
Cook'em

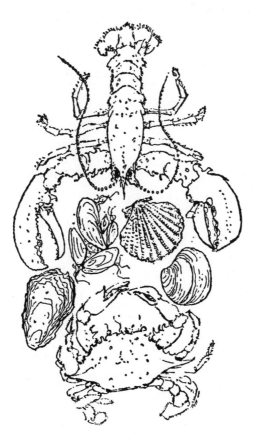

For my men HAROLD, PETER, JOEL

Contents

CONTENTS

Catch'em
and
Cook'em

YOU CAN DO IT TOO!

Some years ago I wrote a series of articles called "Catch 'Em and Cook 'Em" which ran in *Motor Boating* magazine. We had a small cabin cruiser then, *Day Dream*, and so many people threw seafood at me and said, "Frankly, I don't know what to do with it," that I felt sorry for them and tried to put down in writing for them simple and delicious ways to prepare the seafood.

Day Dream has gone long ago and in its place we have a little cottage on an inner creek that flows into the Peconic Bay on eastern Long Island. Every local treasure in the form of shellfish abounds in my little creek, and almost every day I can be found gathering it.

At the edge of the water, right in front of our cottage, at low tide we dig steamers.

Two yards out in the mud, and sometimes in a little sand-bar, quahogs and cherrystones wait to be taken.

In a good year scallops play on the eel grass.

Across the creek, on the edge of the marsh, dwell oysters and mussels.

So in my little pram dinghy, which my son built, I am kept busy in front of my little cottage all summer long, catching the world's most delectable shellfish and then later cooking it inside the cottage.

And still many people come to me and say, "How do you

open those?" and "What do you do with them?" So what interests me now is to share the delight of the shellfish that are so plentiful in front of my cottage.

Oysters are oysters, clams are clams, crabs are crabs, all over the eastern seaboard. But after a recent trip to California, I find there is not too much difference in their shellfish. Many of my methods of catching and cooking shellfish at Towd Point could be deliciously used in San Francisco!

In what follows I have tried to show you not only how to obtain the shellfish, but how to open them, which is the main problem people have after they catch them.

There are many, many recipes about shellfish which you, no doubt, have on your shelves, so I have not tried to list all of them.

Instead I've written simple, easy-to-prepare, delightful recipes that *you* can cook in your own little summer camp or cottage anywhere that shellfish are to be found.

MAKE THE MOST OF GADGETS

To prepare these simple recipes, all you really need is a knife to open the shellfish and a pot to cook them in. But the stores are full of wonderful gadgets to make things easier for you, and to enhance the cooking and serving. So I had some fun browsing around in stores and this is what I came up with.

Clam knife
Clam ram
Scallop knife
Oyster shucker
Oyster knife
Food grinder
Clam steamer (10-quart!)
Shells for baking—Natural clam, crab, and abalone shells that have been dried and cleaned.

Or pottery shells, which are artificial scallop, crab, or clamshells and various-sized casseroles or ramekins.
Outdoor grill
Skewers
Lobster shears (same as poultry)
Lobster crackers
Lobster picks
Tongs

Butter melters
Paper bibs
Decorated platters
Seafood servers
Trivet

COLLECT SPECIAL EQUIPMENT

All you need to gather clams, crabs, oysters, etc. is a strong back, a pail, and a crab net. However, it is fun to add to your equipment and it will increase your take. So here is a list. Good hunting!

Pail
Crab net
Crab trap
Work gloves
Sneakers
Carpenter's apron (to tie around your middle so you can put the clams in the "nail pockets")
Clam fork
Clam rake
Old tire (to float basket or pail)
Lines
Wire
Wire basket (a friend made me a 2′×3′ wire basket of close mesh which I staked in front of the cottage in the shallow water. In this I keep clams and oysters fresh.)
Scallop net
Wooden milk box
Flashlight

Clams

DO YOU KNOW YOUR CLAMS?

Littleneck

This is the hard or round clam when young and small. The size is suitable for eating raw on the half shell. Should be at least an inch and a half across.

Cherrystone

The hard clam when larger than the littleneck; about two inches in diameter.

Quahog

This is the large hard-shell or round clam, at least three inches in diameter. To be used in chowder, stuffed clams, etc.

Steamer

This is the soft or long clam, meaning that the shell is soft and that the clam is elongated, with a black neck. Also called longneck.

DIGGING STEAMERS

At the edge of the water at low tide steamer clams dwell. They reveal themselves to the hunter by tiny holes. If you throw a stone at these holes, the clams will squirt their juice. Immediately fall on your knees and dig with your hands the way a dog uses his paws. Steamers are deep burrowers, so persevere and you will be rewarded by the most delicate-flavored clams of all.

A few years ago there was a wonderful steamer bed right in front of my cottage, and they were just barely under the sand.

Then the next year I could find none. However, that was my fault. I discovered the little round holes and only dug a few inches down, to be disappointed.

What I found out was they had gone down really deep, and I had to go in up to my elbow to bring forth the largest, sweetest, meltiest, tenderest clams going. As with anything else, you have to work for something good.

We make a meal of these, steamed with melted butter, and fresh corn on the cob.

COOKING STEAMERS

STEAMED CLAMS

Wash fresh steamers. Put in saucepan with ½ cup of water. Cover tightly. Steam until all are open. Pour broth in cup; add a chunk of butter and pepper. Dunk clams into melted butter to your heart's desire.

STEAMER CHOWDER

24 steamer clams
½ onion, chopped
3 tablespoons butter
1 quart milk
¼ teaspoon salt
Dash pepper

Steam clams according to directions in preceding recipe, reserving juice. Yellow onion in the butter. Chop clams and add to onion with juice, milk, salt, and pepper. Heat just under the boiling point.

Serves 4.

DIGGING HARD CLAMS

I wish I could tell you just where to find clams, but I can't because they move, tides cover them, dredges destroy them, and clammers get too greedy. But at low tide, search harbors, bays, creeks, and inlets.

I prefer the toe method of getting them. Arm yourself with an old pair of gloves and wear sneakers on your feet. Choose a likely spot and feel around with your toe. If it strikes something hard, investigate with your hands. You might just happen on a bed of clams, as the hard-shells most of the time lie just under the surface of the mud or sand.

This year I learned a new method of digging hard-shell clams, and it can be very effective.

First, tie around your waist a line to which is attached an old-fashioned wooden milk box. Then wade, swim, or row to a nice muddy, weedy clam bed. (This new method came about because the nice sandy beds are being clammed out.)

Get on your hands, knees, and tummy and feel for those elusive hard-shells. This method brings good results, but unless the tide is awfully low, I almost drown, as I'm only 4'11". Besides, I have a horror of mud!

And many people get wonderful results with a rake, and the newest, most modern method is to use diving goggles.

But whatever way you dig them, it will be worth it because there is nothing more soul-satisfying than a really fresh clam.

HOW TO OPEN HARD CLAMS

When you try to open a littleneck or cherrystone clam, you will understand the expression "clam up." If you bruise a little fellow, you might as well put him away for a while; he'll resist you.

First, have the clams cold. This helps to lower their resistance.

Place the clam in the palm of your left hand, the short, fat end nearest your thumb. Place a small knifeblade between the two shells and press with the fingers of the same hand. Then wiggle the knife so the point can cut the muscle, which is down toward the hinge. The clam will loosen. Do the same thing to the top. Then take off the top shell and, with the knife, make sure you've separated all the muscles so you can slurp down the clam.

Some of my clam-digging friends put their haul in a freezer for a while. They claim this helps to open them.

I also have a very non-professional method if I want to eat tight ones immediately. I run them under very hot wa-

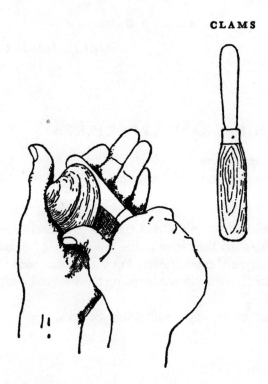

ter for a few seconds. I'm secretly ashamed of this "trick," but I really can't open them a mile a minute the way my son, Joel, does. I wish I could!

Quahogs may be opened the same way or by steaming.

COOKING HARD CLAMS

JEAN'S CLAM APPETIZERS

2 dozen littleneck clams
1 cup dry, seasoned bread stuffing
8 slices of bacon, cut in thirds

Steam open clams. Grind them in a food chopper. Add the clams and their juice to the bread stuffing. If mixture is too runny, add more stuffing. Put the mixture back into the clamshell. Add a sliver of bacon on top and broil until bacon is crisp.

These are wonderful with drinks. Serves 4.

BEN'S CLAM APPETIZERS

Open ½ dozen cherrystones per person.
To each clam add:
A few drops of olive oil
A squeeze of lemon
A dash of black pepper
A sprig of chopped parsley
A dash of garlic salt

Place in a very hot oven or under the broiler and cook until clams are done—about 8 minutes.

CLAMS ON THE HALF SHELL

Littleneck or Cherrystone

½ dozen clams per person
Lemon wedges
Cocktail sauce

Wash and open clams. Serve chilled or on cracked ice with lemon wedges and cocktail sauce.

CLAM JUICE COCKTAIL

1 cup clam juice
1 cup tomato juice
1 teaspoon Worcestershire sauce
2 teaspoons lemon juice

Combine ingredients and chill in the refrigerator until ready to serve.
Serves 4.

BAKED CLAMS

Scrub a mess of hard clams or cherrystones. Place on a grill over a fire of red coals. The clams will open up and cook in their own juice. These are very tasty dipped in melted butter and washed down with the broth from the shell. These can also be done by placing clams in a shallow pan and leaving in a hot (450°) oven until they steam in their juice.
Nice with cocktails.

CLAMS CASINO

8 cherrystone clams per person
½ cup melted butter or olive oil
3 crushed garlic buds
3 tablespoons chopped parsley
1 teaspoon lemon juice
8 half slices of bacon

Soak everything but the clams and bacon together for several hours, letting all the flavors blend well. Open clams either with opener or by steaming. Drain a bit of juice off. On each clam place ½ to 1 teaspoon of the mixture. Place a piece of bacon on top.

Bake in hot oven (450°) for about 10 minutes, or until bacon is crisp and clams plumped.

TOMATO CLAM CHOWDER

1 quart ground clams and juice
¼ pound salt pork, cubed
1 large minced onion
3 minced carrots
4 cubed potatoes
1 16-ounce can tomatoes
1 10½-ounce can condensed tomato soup
2 bay leaves

Fry salt pork and onion until golden. Add clams and juice. Add prepared carrots and potatoes. Last of all, add tomatoes and tomato soup and bay leaves. This procedure is quite different from the one used in making regular clam chowder —so is the smooth consistency and tomatoey flavor.

Serves 4–6.

NEW ENGLAND CLAM CHOWDER

2 dozen or more ground clams and their juice
¼ pound salt pork, diced
1 large onion, diced
4 large boiled potatoes, peeled and diced
1 quart milk
Salt, pepper, flour

Fry salt pork and onion until golden. Add potatoes, barely cover with water, and boil until tender.

Add all but ½ cup of milk. Add seasonings and bring to boiling point. Add clams and broth. Thicken with a little flour blended with the remaining ½ cup of milk. Heat and serve piping hot with pilot crackers and tossed salad. The chowder will improve upon standing.

Serves 4.

LAST-MINUTE NEW ENGLAND CLAM CHOWDER *

1 10½-ounce can minced clams with liquid
1 10½-ounce can frozen potato soup, thawed
1 10½-ounce can light cream
4 tablespoons butter
¼ teaspoon salt
⅛ teaspoon pepper
4 tablespoons chopped chives

Mix all ingredients except chives and heat in a saucepan. Simmer lightly until butter melts.

Serve hot with chopped chives on top.

Serves 4.

* Almost the same as Quick Chowder II.

NEW YORK CLAM CHOWDER

1 dozen large hard clams, chopped, and juice
¼ pound salt pork, chopped
1 onion, chopped
1 cup cubed potatoes
1 carrot, sliced
1 16-ounce can tomatoes
½ teaspoon salt
¼ teaspoon pepper
2 cups hot water
1 teaspoon thyme

Brown pork; add onion and, when yellow, add potatoes, carrots, can tomatoes and salt, pepper, and water. Boil until potatoes and carrots are done. Add clams, thyme, and juice. Simmer for 5 minutes.
Serves 6.

QUICK CHOWDER I

1 dozen or more clams and juice
1 10½-ounce can condensed vegetarian vegetable soup

Chop clams and add with broth to soup.
Heat to boiling point and simmer for a few minutes.
Serves 3–4.

QUICK CHOWDER II

1 7½-ounce can minced clams with juice
1 13-ounce can potato soup (vichyssoise)
1 cup milk
¼ teaspoon salt
⅛ teaspoon pepper
⅛ teaspoon paprika
1 tablespoon butter

Dump all together and simmer gently for a few minutes.
Serves 3–4.

CURRIED CLAMS SOUTHAMPTON

1 can minced clams or 1 cup fresh with juice
1 cup fine bread crumbs
1 teaspoon chopped parsley
1 teaspoon curry powder
Dash of Tabasco sauce
Dash of Worcestershire sauce
Dash of salt and pepper
2 tablespoons mayonnaise

Mix clams, juice, crumbs, parsley, and seasonings with 1
tablespoon of the mayonnaise. Stuff buttered shells with
mixture. Spread remaining mayonnaise on top of each shell
and bake at 425° until mayonnaise is brown and bubbly,
about 15–18 minutes.
Fills three *large* clamshells.

DEVILED CLAMS (REGGIE)

1 dozen clams, chopped and drained
1 beaten egg
1 cup bread crumbs
⅓ cup catsup
1 teaspoon horseradish
¼ teaspoon thyme
½ teaspoon margarine
1 teaspoon minced parsley
1 tablespoon minced onion
1 tablespoon minced celery
¼ teaspoon salt
⅛ teaspoon pepper

Combine all ingredients and mix well. If mixture seems too runny, add more crumbs. Fill shells. Top with buttered crumbs and bake until brown.

Serves 4.

MAMA GEORGIE'S CLAM FRITTERS

1½ dozen clams with juice
Milk
½ cup flour
¼ teaspoon salt
½ teaspoon baking powder
1 egg, beaten

Wash clams and steam open. Chop fine. Drain, reserving juice. Measure clam liquid; add milk to make ¼ cup. Add chopped clams to dry ingredients; add beaten egg and liquid. Drop by spoonfuls into well greased frying pan. Cook until brown on both sides.

Serves 4.

BEN'S CLAM PIE (NORTHPORT)

1 quart clams
3 medium onions
6 medium potatoes
¼ pound salt pork
1 teaspoon sage
1 teaspoon diced celery leaves

Chop clams; dice onions and potatoes. Cut salt pork into small cubes. Fry until crisp. Pour off most of the fat.

Boil clams, onions, and potatoes in quart of liquid (clam juice plus water) for about 20 minutes. Add pork cubes, sage, and celery leaves. Put in baking dish. Cover with crust.

Bake 20 minutes in hot oven.

Serves 4.

RICH CRUST

2 cups flour
2 tablespoons shortening
Enough water to hold it
Pinch of salt

Toss lightly with a fork, then knead a few times on a lightly floured board. Roll out ¼ inch thick.

ITALIAN CLAMS

1 dozen quahog clams, chopped
½ cup clam juice
1 cup bread crumbs
1 crushed garlic clove
¼ teaspoon salt
⅛ teaspoon pepper
1 teaspoon oregano
½ teaspoon basil
½ cup grated Parmesan cheese

Mix everything together except the cheese. Stuff back into the shells and sprinkle the top with cheese. Cook under the broiler until cheese is light brown.
Serves 4.

TOWD POINT CLAM PIE

1 dozen large quahogs and juice
1 large onion
3 tablespoons butter
2 tablespoons flour
1 cup milk
¼ teaspoon salt
⅛ teaspoon pepper
¼ teaspoon paprika

Chop onion and sauté it in butter until yellow; add flour and smooth. Add milk and clam juice and cook until thickened. Chop clams and add with seasonings. Put between unbaked pie crusts and bake in hot oven (450°) until crusts are brown, about 15 to 20 minutes.
Serves 4.

RED CLAM SPAGHETTI

2 cups chopped clams
2 tablespoons olive oil
2 crushed cloves garlic
1 medium onion, chopped
3 stalks celery, chopped
¼ teaspoon thyme
¼ teaspoon basil
¼ teaspoon oregano
¼ teaspoon Italian seasoning (optional)
½ teaspoon salt
⅛ teaspoon pepper
1 16-ounce can tomatoes
1 6-ounce can tomato paste
½ cup water
1 cup or more clam juice. Don't add water.
¼ cup chopped parsley
2 tablespoons butter

Heat oil in pan. Add garlic and onions and cook until transparent. Add celery and seasonings. Add tomatoes, tomato paste, water, clam juice, and parsley. Cook for one hour. Just before serving, add clams and butter.

Serve on spaghetti with Parmesan cheese on top.

Serves 4.

WHITE CLAM SPAGHETTI

1 7½-ounce can minced clams or 1 dozen chopped fresh
    clams and juice
3 tablespoons hot oil
1 diced onion
3 pressed buds of garlic
1 tablespoon flour
½ package of spaghetti

Heat oil (olive or salad) in bottom of pan. Sauté onion
and garlic in this till yellow. Add clams and juice. Smooth
a tablespoon of flour with water and thicken clam sauce.

Pour over enough cooked spaghetti for two.

BRIDGEPORT STUFFED CLAMS

Fresh large quahogs (about 3 per person)
1½ cup soft bread crumbs (if you have more clams, add
    more crumbs)
Salt and pepper to taste
Minced onion, green pepper, pickle, and chopped tomatoes
Bacon

Steam clams open. Remove top shell. Drain off clam broth.
You can prepare this in two ways; both are good.

Either you can chop your clams into your stuffing or leave
them whole and put the stuffing on top. I do it this way for
smaller, tender clams.

Make a mixture of the bread crumbs, salt, pepper, minced
onion, minced green pepper, chopped pickle, and chopped
tomatoes. Moisten this well with the clam liquid. It should
be quite moist and well seasoned.

Stuff clamshell full and put a half a piece of bacon on top of each. Bake in a hot oven (450°) until bacon is crisp and stuffing brown. Everyone will come back for more, and this is one of these dishes you can do in the winter with a can of minced clams.

PECONIC STUFFED CLAMS

15 large quahogs
2 cups seasoned bread stuffing
½ onion, minced
2 teaspoons minced parsley
½ cup chopped tomatoes
1 stalk celery
3 sweet gherkins, chopped
1 teaspoon Worcestershire sauce
2 tablespoons mayonnaise
Dash of Tabasco sauce
Salt and pepper to taste

Steam open and chop clams. Add with the juice to the rest of the ingredients and mix well. Stuff shells, top with bacon, and bake or broil until bacon is done.

Serves 5–6.

SHINNECOCK STUFFED CLAMS

1 dozen quahogs
1½ cups crumbled cheese crackers
¼ cup clam juice
1 tablespoon melted butter
½ minced onion
1 dash Tabasco sauce
1 teaspoon Worcestershire sauce
Salt and pepper to taste

Steam open and chop clams; mix with the cheese crackers. Moisten with their juice and the melted butter. Add the minced onion, Tabasco, Worcestershire sauce, and salt and pepper.

Stuff the mixture back into the shells. Top each with ½ slice of bacon and broil until crisp. Serves 4.

CLAM AND ZUCCHINI SQUASH CASSEROLE

2 dozen littlenecks
2 cups sliced squash
1 8-ounce can spaghetti sauce
Salt and pepper
1 cup bread crumbs
3 tablespoons melted butter

Cook squash (carefully, so it retains its shape) for 8 minutes. Steam open clams.

Place a layer of squash in buttered casserole. Add half the clams and their juice. Repeat. Add spaghetti sauce and seasonings. Mix crumbs and melted butter and top with these.

Bake at 450° for 20 minutes. Serves 4.

Crabs

CRABBING FUN

From late July on, the big "blue claws" run. By the hundreds they pour through the inlets, down the bays, under the bridges and pilings. They are as much fun to catch as to eat.

The equipment is simple—a piece of string, an old fish head or meat, and a crab net. Tie the fish head securely on the string and let it down in a spot where they're running. You'll know where the spot is because you can see them— and other crabbers will be there.

When the crab gets a good hold, pull him gently near the surface; then quickly scoop the net under him. Dump him from the net into your basket. Or if you have to pick him up, do so from the back so that those vicious claws don't get you.

THE CRAB TRAP

Several summers ago I invested in a crab trap. This is a wire contraption with four sides. A piece of cord is attached to each side, and each piece in turn is fastened to a long line in the center. So when the trap is pulled up by the line, the four sides close; when it is lowered to the bottom, the sides open and, of course, the crabs are supposed to stray in, being attracted, naturally, by bait.

So late one lovely afternoon a gang of us headed for Mecox Bay, one of our favorite crabbing spots.

With pieces of string I attached some lovely, old, ripe fish heads to the bottom of the trap and lowered it till it rested on the sand. I counted to sixty, then pulled it up as fast as I could. Two beautiful big, blue-claw crabs were clinging to the fish heads. They were dumped into a basket, and I followed the same procedure again. At the count of sixty I jerked it up and, if I remember correctly, I had three that time. Well, we were beside ourselves with glee and before long we had to stop because we had all we could eat.

I was tenderly folding up the trap when an old man, who had been sitting on a nearby bench watching me, ambled over and said:

"Lady, where did you get that thing? I'm going to get me one and go into the business."

That "thing" is also good to leave tied and lowered from a dock while you tend to other things. Check every once in a while and you may be well rewarded.

WHEN I WAS A LITTLE GIRL

Once a year, when I was a little girl in Maryland, my grandfather used to hire a launch and all the sisters, cousins, uncles, aunts, children, parents, and kin piled in and went down the Sinepuxent Bay for a day's fishing and fun. Many fish were caught. I remember I had a hand line once and a big one nearly pulled me out of the window, but for every fish there were more crabs caught than you could count.

So in the evening when we all arrived home, a big pot was put on the wood fire in the summer kitchen. Water, vinegar, and spices were brought to a boil. With much squealing and laughter, the live crabs were dumped in, not without one or two being spilled on the floor, which caused quite a commotion.

When the crabs were done, they were brought into the dining room, steaming, on huge platters. Cold glasses of beer soon appeared with pickles, cheese, and crackers, and everyone dove into the most wonderful feast ever. I was half asleep on someone's knee, but I can still taste those sweet crabs.

Nowadays, it would be a good idea to use a plastic cloth.

NIGHTTIME CRABBING

More recently, my boys I think will always remember one night several summers ago when someone said, "I'm hungry for crabs."

Before long, nets, string, baskets, fish heads, flashlights, and people piled into cars and headed for the Shinnecock canal. It was a beautiful summer night, but the most beautiful sight that greeted us was hundreds of large blue-claw crabs swimming next to the locks.

Night crabbing is great fun and different from daytime. If you shine a light on a crab, he will be attracted by it. Then, when you get his attention, you draw the light toward the bulkhead and he will follow it. Then all you have to do is to get the net under him and scoop him up.

That particular night the crabs were just itching to be

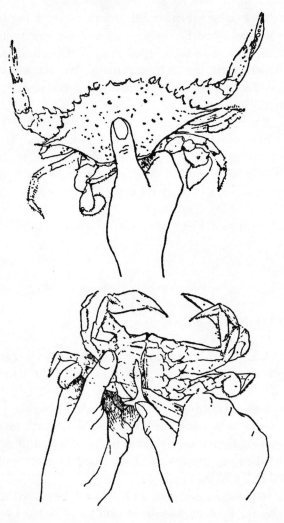

caught so, in no time at all, baskets were filled. However, in his eagerness to get an especially large one, my teen-age son, Joel, who was a good man with the net, fell in. Fortunately the crabs were afraid of him, and he got out unscathed.

Family, friends, and relations all went home, put a large pot on the gas stove with water, vinegar, and spices, and dumped the crabs in, not without spilling one or two.

We also had large glasses of cold beer, pickles, cheese, and crackers—and celebrated another memorable crab feast.

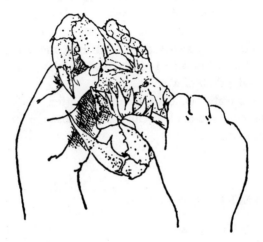

CLEANING CRABS

Cook and cool a live crab.

Turn it over so that the apron side is up. The apron is the underside, which has a design like an apron. With a sharp knife lift up the apron and tear it off. With knife, clean out lungs under the eyes. Peel off the "devil fingers"—the long, spongelike substance on each side under the topshell. Some people like to wash off the brown and green fat. Break the crab in half, crack the large claws, and you are ready for eating or picking out the meat for your favorite recipe.

COOKING CRABS

SPICED CRABS (CRAB BOIL)

Bring a large pot of water to boil on a hot fire. Add about a half cup of vinegar and a teaspoon of salt and a teaspoon of a mixed spice called Shrimp or Crab Boil.

Throw in a mess of the largest blue-claw crabs you can catch. Cook at a fast boil from 5 to 10 minutes. Drain.

If you can't buy a package of Crab Boil, the nearest I can figure out is to throw in a pinch of whole cloves, several bay leaves, and a dash of allspice.

Pick the crabs hot; dunk in melted butter.

Or eat cold and dunk in chive mayonnaise.

Or just *eat.*

STEAMED CRABS

1 dozen blue claws
½ cup vinegar
Water
3 bay leaves
¼ teaspoon whole cloves

Pour the vinegar and water to a depth of one inch in a large, heavy pot fitted with a trivet for steaming. Add the bay leaves and cloves and bring it to a boil. Dump the crabs into the trivet and steam for 10 minutes. Drain, cool, and clean them. Crack the claws; break the crabs in half and serve on a large platter. These with corn on the cob make a wonderful meal.

Serves 4–6.

STRONG COTTAGE CRAB APPETIZERS

1 cup fresh crab meat
2 tablespoons mayonnaise
1 teaspoon curry powder
¼ teaspoon salt
⅛ teaspoon pepper
½ teaspoon Worcestershire sauce

Mix all ingredients together. Serve on crackers.
The gang next door served these and ate them with their cocktails while they watched the beautiful sunsets over Holmes' Hill.
Serves 4.

CRAB CAKE

2 cups flaked crab meat, fresh or canned
¼ teaspoon salt
⅛ teaspoon pepper
Dash Worcestershire sauce
1 egg, slightly beaten
Flour

Mix crab meat, salt, pepper, Worcestershire sauce, and egg. Shape into small cakes. Chill for several hours. When ready to cook, dredge with flour and fry in hot, deep fat for 2 to 3 minutes, or until light brown. Can also be sautéed in sweet butter. In deep fat, it's advisable to use a basket.
Serves 4.

DOTTIE'S CRAB CAKE

1 pound fresh crab meat (backfin, if possible)
2 tablespoons chopped parsley
1 teaspoon Worcestershire sauce
1 tablespoon mayonnaise
2 tablespoons (or less) cream
1 beaten egg
Salt and pepper to taste
Bread crumbs

Mix all ingredients except bread crumbs. Shape into cakes. Keep cold for several hours. Dredge in bread crumbs and sauté until brown.

Makes about 8 large cakes.

CRABS CREOLE

2 cups crab meat
1 large onion, chopped
1 crushed clove garlic
½ cup chopped green pepper
4 tablespoons bacon fat
1 16-ounce can tomatoes
½ cup chopped celery
1 teaspoon sugar
1 teaspoon Worcestershire sauce
Dash Tabasco sauce
½ teaspoon salt
⅛ teaspoon pepper

Sauté onion, garlic, and green pepper in bacon fat until tender. Add everything else and simmer for 20 minutes. Serve on rice. Serves 4.

CRAB BISQUE

1 6½-ounce can crab meat, or 1 cup fresh
1 10½-ounce can condensed tomato soup
1 10½-ounce can condensed green pea soup
1 10½-ounce can water
1 10½-ounce can milk
¼ teaspoon salt
⅛ teaspoon pepper

Combine everything and heat. Don't cook too long.
Serves 6.

DEVILED CRABS

1 cup crab meat (fresh or canned)
1 cup bread crumbs
½ cup minced celery
1 egg, slightly beaten
½ cup minced green pepper
1 teaspoon prepared mustard
1 tablespoon Worcestershire sauce
¼ teaspoon pepper
½ teaspoon salt
Dash of Tabasco
2 tablespoons lemon juice
½ cup melted butter or margarine

Mix ingredients together well and stuff into crab shells or
individual baking dishes. Place in hot oven (375°) for about
12 to 15 minutes.
Serves 2–3.

CRAB MEAT AU GRATIN

1 6½-ounce can crab meat or 1 cup fresh crab meat
2 cups white sauce
1 cup grated sharp cheese
Salt and pepper to taste
1 teaspoon Worcestershire sauce

Mix white sauce and crab meat. Add cheese. Season with a touch of salt, pepper, and Worcestershire sauce.

Stuff buttered crab shells or individual baking dishes. Pop into 425° oven; bake until golden brown.

This is also delicious when you omit the cheese; add 2 tablespoons of sherry instead. Cover the top with buttered crumbs or mayonnaise and bake at 425° for 10 to 15 minutes.   Serves 4.

MARYLAND CRAB IMPERIAL

2 cups backfin crab meat
4 tablespoons melted butter
¼ onion, chopped
4 teaspoons chopped fresh parsley
1 tablespoon mayonnaise
2 tablespoons cream
1 teaspoon Worcestershire sauce
Salt and pepper to taste

Sauté onion in butter.

Mix all ingredients well. Pile into crab shells or individual baking dishes. Spread extra mayonnaise on top.

Bake at 350° for ½ hour.

Serves 4.

CRAB GUMBO (SOUTHERN)

2 dozen large blue crabs
1 medium onion, chopped
1 green pepper
1 tablespoon butter or bacon fat
1 tablespoon flour
1 16-ounce can tomatoes
Salt and pepper to taste
1 teaspoon sugar
1 15½-ounce can okra or 1 package frozen
¼ teaspoon celery salt
1 bay leaf

Boil crabs, drain, and clean. Break into halves or quarters. Fry onions and green peppers in fat until golden. Add flour and stir until brown. Add tomatoes, salt, pepper, sugar, okra, celery salt, and bay leaf. Heat crabs thoroughly in this mixture and serve with rice on the side.
Serves 6.

CRAB NEWBURG

1 6½-ounce can crab meat or 1 cup fresh
2 cups white sauce
3 tablespoons sherry
½ teaspoon salt
⅛ teaspoon pepper
1 teaspoon prepared mustard
1 teaspoon Worcestershire sauce

Mix all together and heat gently. Serve on toast points.
Serves 4.

CRAB RAVIGOTE

1 6½-ounce can crab meat (or 1 cup fresh)
¼ teaspoon salt
⅛ teaspoon pepper
⅛ teaspoon cayenne pepper
1 teaspoon prepared mustard
1 tablespoon oil
½ tablespoon chopped parsley
1 tablespoon chopped celery
1 hard-cooked egg, chopped
3 tablespoons vinegar

Season crab meat with salt, pepper, cayenne, and mustard. Add remaining ingredients. Put in crab shells; spread evenly with mayonnaise and serve very cold. Delicious!
Serves 2.

CRAB SPECIAL

1 6½-ounce can crab meat or 1 cup fresh
1 tablespoon mayonnaise
1 tablespoon green pepper, minced
1 tablespoon red pepper, minced
¼ teaspoon salt
⅛ teaspoon pepper
1 teaspoon Worcestershire sauce
1 egg, slightly beaten

Mix everything together and stuff into shells. Spread extra mayonnaise on each. Bake at 425° for 10–15 minutes.
Serves 3.

CRAB MEAT À LA RECTOR

1 cup crab meat
½ green pepper, diced
½ medium onion, diced
1 16-ounce can tomatoes
½ teaspoon Worcestershire sauce
¼ teaspoon salt
⅛ teaspoon pepper
1 teaspoon sugar
2 hard-cooked eggs, sliced
1 cup bread crumbs
2 tablespoons butter

Mix the green pepper, onion, tomatoes, crab meat, seasonings, and sugar together. Spread mixture in a buttered casserole. Layer sliced eggs next. Top with crumbs and dot with butter. Bake at 300° for one hour.
Serves 4.

CRAB MEAT AND SMITHFIELD HAM

1 cup crab meat
2 medium slices Smithfield ham or smoked ham
2 tablespoons butter

Sauté the ham in the butter. Put aside and keep warm while you sauté the crab meat in the same pan for about 3 minutes. Serve the crab meat on the ham.
Serves 2.

STUFFED CRABS

4 large crabs
1 cup bread crumbs
6 tablespoons butter, melted
½ onion, chopped
1 teaspoon parsley
¼ teaspoon salt
⅛ teaspoon pepper
¼ teaspoon sage
¼ teaspoon thyme
2 teaspoons mayonnaise
¼ teaspoon paprika

Boil and clean crabs.

Mix the bread crumbs, melted butter, onion, and seasonings together. Stuff the cavities of the crabs with this mixture. Spread them evenly with mayonnaise and sprinkle the paprika on top. Bake at 350° for 25 minutes.

Serves 4.

CRAB SOUP

2 short ribs of beef
2 quarts water
1 tablespoon salt
2 carrots, diced
½ small head of cabbage, chopped
1 large onion, chopped
½ bunch celery, diced
½ bunch parsley, chopped

6 boiled blue-claw crabs
½ package frozen corn
½ package frozen lima beans
½ package frozen peas
¼ cup barley

Cook the first eight ingredients for one hour. Add the rest of the ingredients and cook for ½ hour. Before serving, remove crab aprons and clean the crabs, break them in half, remove the meat from the claws, and add to soup.

Serves 12.

CRAB MEAT WITH WALNUTS

2 cups picked crab meat
½ cup chopped walnuts
1 hard-cooked egg, chopped
2 tablespoons parsley
½ teaspoon salt
⅛ teaspoon pepper
1 teaspoon Worcestershire sauce
½ teaspoon prepared mustard
Dash Tabasco sauce
¾ cup mayonnaise

Mix all ingredients together except ¼ cup mayonnaise. Spoon into crab shells or baking shells. Spread remaining mayonnaise on top of each. Bake at 400° for 25 minutes.

Fills 4–6 shells.

CRAB MEAT AND SHRIMP

8 extra-large jumbo shrimp, cleaned
1 cup crab meat
1 tablespoon mayonnaise
1 teaspoon chopped parsley
½ teaspoon salt
⅛ teaspoon pepper
1 egg
1 tablespoon water
1 cup fine bread crumbs

Cut three quarters of the way through the shrimp. Mix the crab meat with the mayonnaise, parsley, salt, and pepper and fill the shrimp cavities with this mixture. Beat egg with water and dip each filled shrimp into the mixture. Roll in bread crumbs. Fry in a basket in deep fat for 3 to 4 minutes. Ambrosia!

Serves 3–4.

SOFT-SHELL CRABS

A soft-shell crab is one which is molting, or shedding its hard shell. They are usually available only from June until September and not terribly plentiful at that, as you have to catch the crab at just the exact moment he's undressed. They are considered a great delicacy.

"Softies" are usually quite lethargic, and you can pick them up from the bottom on a day when the water is clear—or one might happen to stroll into your trap if you're real lucky.

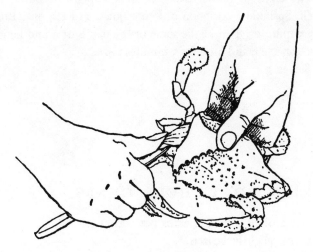

CLEANING SOFT-SHELL CRABS

You can handle a live soft-shell crab because it's not its usual scrappy self. Remove the apron and clean out the lung-like substance under the eyes. Then with a sharp knife probe under the top shell and scrape out the "devil fingers," the long, spongy stuff. You're all set then.

COOKING SOFT-SHELL CRABS

BROILED SOFT-SHELL CRABS

4 large soft-shell crabs
4 tablespoons butter
4 teaspoons lemon juice

Lay crabs in broiler pan. Put a tablespoon of butter on
each. Sprinkle a teaspoon of lemon juice on each one. Broil
for 5 minutes. Turn, ladle some of the pan butter and lemon
juice on each, and broil for 5 minutes more.

Serves 4.

FRIED SOFT-SHELL CRABS

Use 2 small soft-shell crabs per person.
1 egg, slightly beaten
¼ cup water
½ cup flour or ½ cup cracker crumbs
Fat for frying

Mix egg and water. Dip the crabs in this mixture then roll
in the flour or cracker crumbs. Have hot fat a half inch deep
in a skillet. Fry for 10 minutes.

Serve on toast with lemon wedges and tartare sauce.

SAUTÉED SOFT-SHELL CRABS

1 large soft-shell crab or 2 small ones per person
½ cup butter

Melt the butter in a skillet. Sauté the crab for 5 minutes. Turn and sauté 5 minutes more, or until golden brown. Serve on a slice of toast with a sliver of lemon and tartare sauce on the side.

Lobsters

BUYING LOBSTERS

Someday there will be lobsters in my little creek, because several times I have seen tiny baby lobsters, but in the meantime I have to buy them.

My neighbors and I often have a jaunt to Montauk to pick out the fresh ones for a beach feast, but fortunately we can always buy wonderful ones right in town, and in June they are the fattest and least expensive.

And so it is all along the eastern seaboard: one can buy the best, freshest lobsters—except on the Maine coast, where I understand people have lobster pots instead of lawns!

I think the best eating lobsters weigh 1½ to 2 pounds. They are tender, sweet, and satisfying.

However, one day I sent my son, Joel, out to buy some for a party and, to my dismay, he came home with a 10-pound one. After much fussing we borrowed a new garbage pail and boiled him. He was delicious!

Make sure you purchase a live, wiggling lobster, and don't be afraid. The claws are usually pegged. Keep it in a cool place until ready to prepare.

CLEANING LOBSTERS

For lobster broil, place a *live* lobster on its back on a cutting board. With your left hand hold the head down and with your right plunge a sharp knife in the top of the dividing line and split all the way to the tail. With both hands crack open. Remove the intestines and the sac under the head.

If the red stuff is there, keep it in or use it in a stuffing. It's the roe, or coral, and it's very good. The green stuff is good also. It is called tomalley.

For steaming or boiling a lobster, hold it by the back of the head and plunge it into boiling water. Don't be squeamish; the result is worth the trouble.

After you steam or boil a lobster, clean it the same way as a live one.

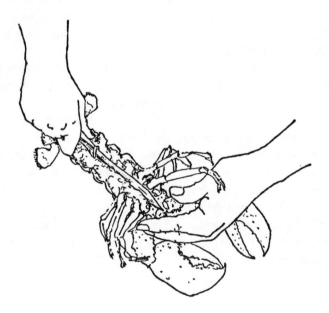

COOKING LOBSTERS

BOILED LOBSTERS

1- to 1½-pound lobster per person
Large kettle of boiling water.

Plunge lobster quickly into rapidly boiling water. Cover tightly and boil 20 minutes.
Remove and split and clean.
Serve hot with melted butter and lemon juice, or serve cold with mayonnaise.

BROILED LOBSTER

1- to 2-pound lobster per person
1½ cup stuffing per lobster (see lobster stuffings)
Melted butter
Lemon juice
Lemon wedges

If you are going to broil the lobsters soon after you purchase them, your fishman can split and clean them for you. Otherwise, split and clean your lobsters.
Fill the cavity with a stuffing of your choice and brush melted butter over the flesh. Sprinkle lemon juice over this.
Place on a broiler, flesh side to the flame, about 2 to 3 inches away. Cook for about 10 minutes, basting every 5 minutes with melted butter. Flesh should be nice and white when done, and tender when tested with a fork. When in doubt, allow a few more minutes.
Serve with melted butter and lemon wedges.

CHARCOAL-BROILED LOBSTER

1- to 2-pound lobster per person
Plenty of melted butter
½ cup lemon juice
Red-coal charcoal fire

Place split and cleaned lobsters shell side down on the grill over a hot fire. Brush the flesh with melted butter and sprinkle this with lemon juice. Broil for 10 minutes. Turn fast and broil shell side about 6 minutes. Turn up again and brush with melted butter. They should be done, but test with fork; flesh should separate easily. Serve with the rest of the melted butter and lemon juice.

We love to have this feast on the beach by the ocean.

We use paper plates for the lobster and paper cups for the melted butter and lemon juice.

The scent of the salt air, mingled with the charcoal smoke and lobster aroma, almost drives one crazy with hunger.

MAINE STEAMED LOBSTERS

1- to 1½-pound lobster per person
1 inch water in a large pan

Plunge lobsters in steaming water quickly to kill them.
Cover and steam 20 minutes.

Take out, clean, and serve with lemon juice and melted butter.

My husband was squeamish about this method. However, I learned it from a friend who spends all her summers in Maine and I must say the lobsters are always tender and delicious.

LOBSTER ROLLS

1 cup lobster meat
6 tablespoons butter
3 tablespoons sherry
¼ teaspoon salt
⅛ teaspoon pepper
1 teaspoon Worcestershire sauce
2 buttered and toasted hamburger rolls

Melt butter. Sauté lobster in it for a few minutes. Add sherry and seasonings and serve on hot, toasted rolls.
Serves 2.

VERA'S LOBSTER ROLLS

1 6½-ounce can or 1 cup chopped lobster meat
½ cup cubed Swiss cheese
2 tablespoons minced onion
¼ teaspoon salt
¼ cup mayonnaise
1 teaspoon vinegar
4 hamburger buns

Toss everything together. Spread hamburger buns with butter. Then spread with lobster mixture. Wrap each bun in foil. Bake at 350° for 20 minutes. Cool for 5 minutes before opening. Wonderful for lunch!
Serves 4.

JAN'S LOBSTER WITH CLAM JUICE

1 lobster per person
2 cups fresh or bottled clam juice

Heat clam juice in a large heavy kettle. Plunge lobsters in head down. Cover tightly.
Steam for 20 minutes.

LOBSTER SAUCE

1 cup lobster meat
2 cups medium cream sauce
½ teaspoon salt
⅛ teaspoon pepper
1 teaspoon Worcestershire sauce
2 tablespoons sherry

Add lobster, seasonings, and sherry to the cream sauce.
Heat through.
Wonderful served on rolls.
Wonderful to dip toast points in at a cocktail party.
On rolls serves 4.
For cocktails serves 8.

LOBSTER STUFFINGS

CLAM STUFFING

1 cup bread crumbs
½ cup chopped clams
½ cup clam juice

Mix everything together and stuff back into shell. Enough for two 1- to 2-pound lobsters.

CORAL STUFFING

1 cup bread crumbs
4 tablespoons melted butter
Salt and pepper to taste
Coral (red) and tomalley (green stuff) from lobster

Mix everything together and stuff back into shell cavity. I think this is the best stuffing ever. Unfortunately, you don't always have the coral, which is the roe in a female lobster.
This amount stuffs 2 lobsters.

PLAIN STUFFING

1 cup bread crumbs
4 tablespoons melted butter
Salt and pepper to taste

Mix everything together and stuff into lobster cavity.
This amount should stuff about two 1- to 1½-pound lobsters.

CRAB MEAT STUFFING

1 cup bread crumbs
½ cup crab meat
4 tablespoons melted butter
Salt and pepper to taste
Dash Worcestershire sauce

Mix everything together and stuff into lobster shell.
Enough for two 1- to 2-pound lobsters.

Mussels

HOW TO GATHER AND PREPARE THEM

Across the creek from our little cottage grow the most abundant, most delectable, and most neglected mollusks— the mussels.

I can thank my brother for introducing me to these blue-black beauties many years ago aboard his boat.

Few people know about mussels, especially Americans. But speak to a Frenchman or a Belgian and he will go into ecstasies.

I have only a few recipes for mussels, compared to the number I have for clams, but each year I add one more recipe and I always think it is the best.

Blue-black mussels cling to rocks, wharves, and mud. It is best to pick them at low tide because the fresh, live ones would be exposed at that time. Mussels cling by means of a beard. So when you pull a mussel from its home, be sure there is some resistance and that some of the beard is still visible. The beard is a sign that the mussel is alive.

Dead mussels, which become filled with mud, abound. They are the same weight as live mussels and pressure on the shells with the thumb does not always open them. I call these fakes "mudders." Fortunately, if you get one in the pot by mistake, it will not open by itself and spill out the mud.

The only way to gather mussels is to pull them off by hand, and experience will soon show you the perfect ones.

They need stiff scrubbing with a wire brush, and you must pull off the beard.

HOW TO OPEN MUSSELS

The only method I know to open mussels is to steam them. Put them in a large pot with ¼ cup of water. If by any chance one or several remain closed after steaming, do not investigate. Throw them away immediately, because they will contain mud (but fortunately these will not open and spill in the pan).

COOKING MUSSELS

STEAMED MUSSELS

Scrub and unbeard mussels.
Place in pot with ¼ cup of white wine, preferably Chablis.
Steam until open.
Serve with the broth and with melted butter on the side.
If these are the main dish, I suggest at least 1 dozen per person.

MUSSEL APPETIZER VINAIGRETTE

24 mussels
4 tablespoons vinegar
¼ teaspoon salt
⅛ teaspoon pepper
6 tablespoons olive oil
1 tablespoon chopped green pepper
1 tablespoon chopped pickle
1 tablespoon chopped parsley
1 teaspoon sugar
1 tablespoon chopped chives or scallions

Clean and steam open mussels and let cool.
Remove cooled mussels from the shells. Mix all other ingredients together and chill the mussels in the mixture in the refrigerator for several hours.
Serve very cold in a platter with a bowl of crackers on the side.
Serves 4.

MUSSELS IN BACON

24 mussels
1/4 cup water
12 slices bacon
4 tablespoons parsley

Scrub and beard mussels. Steam open in a kettle with the water.

Remove from shell. Wrap a half slice of bacon around each mussel. Broil until bacon is done, turning once. Serve on buttered toast with a sprinkling of parsley on top.

Serves 4.

BELGIAN MUSSELS

4 dozen mussels
1 minced onion
1 minced garlic bud
1 tablespoon bacon fat
1 tablespoon butter
1 tablespoon olive oil
1/2 cup white wine
3 tablespoons chopped parsley

Cook onion and garlic in the bacon fat, butter, and olive oil until onions are yellow. Add mussels. Pour wine over mussels and add chopped parsley. Steam until mussels open wide—about 20 minutes.

Serves 3-4.

ROUX

2 egg yolks
2 tablespoons cream

Beat egg yolks and cream with a fork. Add 1 cup of broth from the steamed mussels. Stir until thick over low fire or double boiler, being careful not to overcook. Add more broth if needed. Serve mussels with top shell removed and the roux poured on top.

Serves 3–4.

FRENCH MUSSELS

1 dozen mussels per person
1 chopped shallot
¼ cup Chablis
Pinch thyme
⅛ teaspoon ground pepper
2 tablespoons chopped fresh parsley
2 tablespoons butter
1½ tablespoons flour

Scrub and unbeard mussels. Place in pot with wine, herbs, and seasoning, and steam until shells open. Then remove the top shells and place mussels on a large platter.

In another pan melt the butter and add the flour; make into a paste. Carefully add the stock from the mussels, stirring constantly until the sauce is the consistency of a thin gravy. Pour the sauce over the mussels.

Serve these with French bread so that you can sop up this wonderful juice.

ITALIAN MUSSELS

3 dozen mussels
3 tablespoons olive oil
1 teaspoon chopped hot red pepper
3 crushed garlic cloves
3 tablespoons chopped parsley
½ teaspoon oregano

Heat olive oil and sauté chopped peppers and garlic for a few minutes. Add mussels, chopped parsley, and oregano. A spot of red wine adds to the flavor and helps start the steaming. Cover and steam until opened.

This can be served hot or chilled.

Serves 3.

DAVIS CREEK STUFFED MUSSELS

2 dozen mussels
3 tablespoons butter
½ medium onion, minced fine
1 tablespoon chopped parsley
½ teaspoon sage
¼ teaspoon salt
⅛ teaspoon pepper
1½ cups bread crumbs

Clean and steam open the mussels. Remove the top shell. Sauté the onion in the butter until the onion is yellow. Dump in everything else and mix well. Spread the stuffing over each mussel in its half shell and put under the broiler for a few minutes, or until the top is light brown.

Serves 2–4.

MUSSELS MARINARA

Use at least 1 dozen mussels per person.
Scrub and unbeard mussels.
Place in pot and pour over them one 8-ounce can of marinara sauce.
Steam until open.
Serve over spaghetti with Italian bread on the side.

MUSSELS À LA RUSSE

2 dozen mussels
1 cup mayonnaise
½ cup chili sauce

Clean and steam open the mussels. Cool and remove from their shells. Mix the mayonnaise and chili sauce. Add the mussels to this mixture and chill well. Serve on a bed of lettuce as an appetizer or salad.

Serves 4.

Oysters

I will always be reminded of one bright, cold March day when, driving back to New York from Southampton, my neighbor and I stopped at the Shinnecock canal to buy some fresh flounders.

The fishman, who sells from an old boat there, tried to persuade me to buy some oysters.

To his amazement and that of a couple standing nearby, Elise Flanagan and I cried, "Oysters? Buy oysters? Why, we have a bushelful right in this car." And to prove it we held up several huge ones.

The eyes of the men nearly popped out, and they promptly wanted to know where we got them. "Oh," we said casually, "right in front of our cottage."

"Well," said one, "I'll tell you what I'll do. I'll come and help you dig them and I'll give you half."

"No thank you, sir. We don't even have to dig them. We just pick them up."

Which was true.

On that particular day we had driven to check a robbery in the cottage. Naturally we went out front to look at the water, and there was a phenomenally low tide—lower than we had ever seen—and flats undiscovered by us were exposed. Lying in the mud with the lips just barely showing were dozens of oysters.

We immediately pounced on them and took home a bushel of the most delicious oysters we ever ate.

It's never happened again, I might add.

GATHERING OYSTERS

At low tide one can see the succulent oysters clinging to the mudbanks in the marshes. Sometimes they are just above the water, sometimes just under. Float along in a rowboat and pull them from the banks. If the water is extra clear—and it is very often unusually clear in September, when it is permissible to gather them—the lips of the deep ones can be seen open for air. It is advisable to use gloves because the edges of the oysters are sometimes very sharp.

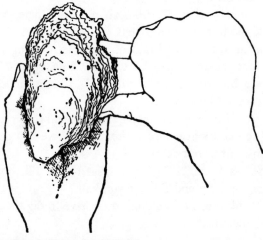

HOW TO OPEN OYSTERS

Place the oyster mound side down. If you look at one oyster sideways, you'll notice one side is fatter than the other; this I call the mound.

With a hammer or oyster opener hammer off the excess lip until you see a slight opening. Force tip of knife into opening and slide it up and under till you can slice the muscle. Do the same on the upper side. Take off upper shell and there you leave the oyster ready for anything—especially eating!

COOKING OYSTERS

OYSTERS ON THE HALF SHELL

Oysters—½ dozen per person
Ice
Cocktail sauce

Wash oysters and chill thoroughly. Open and serve on cracked ice with cocktail sauce and saltines.

ROASTED OYSTERS

Oysters in shell—½ dozen per person
Wash oysters thoroughly and chip shells.
Place in oven pan and cook in 450° oven until open. It takes about 20 minutes.
Remove top shell and serve in the deep half.
Good with salt, pepper, and lemon juice.
Good with vinegar sauce.
Good with cocktail sauce.
Good with cocktails!

ROBINS ISLAND OYSTERS

1 pint cleaned oysters and juice
2 tablespoons butter
½ cup medium cream
¼ teaspoon nutmeg
2 tablespoons sherry
¼ teaspoon salt
⅛ teaspoon pepper

Sauté oysters in the butter for a few minutes. Add cream, nutmeg, sherry, salt, and pepper. Warm through (do not boil) and serve on toast.

Serves 3–4.

SAUTÉED OYSTERS

1 dozen oysters
2 tablespoons butter
½ cup thin cream
1 teaspoon chopped parsley
¼ teaspoon salt
⅛ teaspoon pepper
Dash Tabasco sauce

Melt butter; add oysters and cook until edges curl. Then add cream, parsley, and seasonings and stir until warm. Serve on toast.

Serves 2.

SCAI LOPED OYSTERS

1 pint oysters with their liquor
1 cup cracker crumbs
¼ teaspoon salt
⅛ teaspoon pepper
½ cup butter
1 cup medium cream
½ teaspoon nutmeg
½ teaspoon Worcestershire sauce
2 or 3 drops Tabasco sauce
1 cup bread crumbs

In a buttered casserole put a layer of cracker crumbs; cover with half the oysters. Sprinkle with salt and pepper, and dot with butter and half the cream, nutmeg, Worcestershire sauce and 1 drop of Tabasco. Cover with the bread crumbs and repeat the oyster mixture, adding the rest of the cream, liquor, and seasonings. Lastly, cover with the remaining crumbs, dot with butter, and bake 30 minutes at 400°.
Serves 4.

OYSTER STEW

1 pint oysters with their liquor
1 quart milk with top milk
¼ teaspoon salt
⅛ teaspoon pepper
4 tablespoons butter

Cook oysters in their liquor until the edges curl. Add milk, salt, pepper, and butter, and heat to just under boiling point or milk will curdle. Serve with large oyster crackers.
Serves 4.

OYSTERS IN WHITE WINE

1 pint oysters
1 cup white wine
¼ teaspoon salt
⅛ teaspoon pepper
1 onion, sliced
1 tablespoon parsley
1 bay leaf
½ teaspoon thyme

In a saucepan or chafing dish bring the white wine with seasonings and herbs to a simmer. Add the oysters and cook gently until the edges curl.
Serves 3.

STEAMED OYSTERS

Oysters in shell—½ dozen per person
½ cup water
½ teaspoon Worcestershire sauce
½ teaspoon lemon juice

Wash oysters.
Chip excess shell off the end of each oyster.
Place in kettle. Add water, Worcestershire sauce, and lemon juice. Put cover on tightly and steam until open. It takes about 15 minutes.
Remove top shells and serve on a platter with a sauce of your choice on the side. I recommend cocktail sauce, or hot butter sauce, or plain melted butter.

FRIED OYSTERS

1 pint oysters
1 egg
1 tablespoon water
1 cup fine bread crumbs
Salt and pepper to taste

Drain oysters and pat dry with a paper towel. Beat egg
with water and add salt and pepper to taste. Dip each oyster
into this mixture and roll in crumbs. Place the oysters in a
wire basket and deep-fat-fry for 3 to 4 minutes. Or fry in
shallow fat and turn once after 2 minutes.

Serve on a platter with tartare sauce, lemon wedges, chili
sauce, and cole slaw. Serves 2–3.

I love the large Chincoteague oysters. However, they are
not easily obtainable, so I put two oysters together and dip
them into the egg mixture and bread crumbs *twice*. This
holds them together.

Scallops

HOW TO GET THEM

On the sixteenth of September there is a change on the Peconic Bay, and in all the little harbors, inlets, and creeks that are in the area. For on that day it is legal to take those tiny, sweet, tender bay scallops for which the Peconic is famous.

Every man, woman, boy, and girl who can get out on the water is there. They pick up the scallops with nets of every shape and form; they pick them up with their hands, when the tide is low enough and when it is a plentiful year. They are easy to get because they lie on the mud, sand, or weeds. The gulls join the people in scalloping, and they know where to find the largest.

HOW TO OPEN SCALLOPS

Place the scallop in your left hand, dark side down. Insert the blade of a knife (you can buy a scallop knife if you wish) in the hinge. Scoop the knife 'way down in the fat area in the bottom. Cut the muscle; then do the same on the top. Open. Pull the little white muscle from the rest of the scallop. That is your pearl. After you do a pail of these, you will not be greedy—because a half a bushel yields about one quart. But it is worth it.

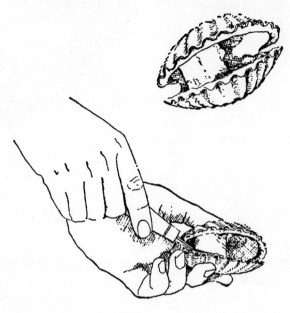

COOKING SCALLOPS

BROILED SCALLOPS

2 cups bay scallops
6 tablespoons melted butter
Juice from half lemon
½ teaspoon salt
¼ teaspoon pepper

Stir scallops in the melted butter until they are coated. Spread them out in a broiler. Broil for 10 minutes or until brown; sprinkle with the lemon juice and turn every few minutes so that they will brown evenly.

Serves 3–4.

SCALLOPS EN BROCHETTE

2 cups scallops
8 slices bacon
½ pound mushrooms

Wash and dry scallops. Cut bacon slices in thirds. Cut ends off mushrooms. Put a piece of bacon on the skewer first, a scallop next, then a mushroom cap. Continue this till skewer is filled. Brush with oil and broil over a white-coal fire until light brown. Or place on your broiling pan and broil, or, if you're lucky enough, broil in your electric broiler.

We like to do this outside while we enjoy the sunset.

SAUTÉED SCALLOPS

1 pint bay scallops
4 tablespoons butter
Toast points

I think that scallops have such a wonderful, delicate, elusive flavor of their own that they are best prepared in the simplest way.

Melt the butter in a pan and sauté the scallops until light golden. If they are truly fresh, a liquid will come from them. Pour the scallops and their juice over toast points. You might serve a lemon wedge.

Serves 3–4.

FRIED SCALLOPS

1 pint scallops
4 tablespoons bacon fat
½ cup flour

Roll scallops in flour. Heat fat about ½ inch deep in pan.
Fry scallops until golden brown. Serve with tartare sauce
and lemon. It only takes about 8 to 10 minutes.
Serves 3–4.

SCALLOPED SCALLOPS

1 pint bay scallops
1 cup cracker crumbs
1 cup top milk or medium cream
½ cup butter
½ teaspoon salt
⅛ teaspoon pepper
⅛ teaspoon nutmeg
1 cup bread crumbs

Put layer of cracker crumbs in a buttered casserole. Cover
with the scallops; add half the cream; dot with butter; sprinkle with salt, pepper, and nutmeg. Add the bread crumbs and
cover with the rest of the cream and butter. Bake at 350°
for 30 minutes.
Serves 4 generously.

SOUTHAMPTON SCALLOPS

2 cups bay scallops
½ medium onion, minced, or 2 tablespoons chopped
  chives
2 tablespoons butter
1 10½-ounce can condensed cream of mushroom soup
2 tablespoons milk
1 teaspoon Worcestershire sauce
Dash cayenne pepper
¼ teaspoon salt
⅛ teaspoon pepper
½ cup grated Parmesan cheese

Sauté onion or chives gently in butter until yellow. Add
the can of mushroom soup. Measure 2 tablespoons of milk
and stir into the soup. Add the seasonings and scallops. Simmer softly for 10 minutes. Pack into individual baking shells.
Sprinkle with Parmesan cheese. Brown under broiler.
  Serves 4–6.

SCALLOPS WITH SAUCES

Scallops—at least ½ dozen per person
Open scallops and chill for several hours in the refrigerator.
Serve chilled with lemon juice
                or
          cocktail sauce
                or
          melted butter
This is the way the "natives" like them.

SCALLOPS WITH WINE

1 pint scallops
4 tablespoons butter
½ cup white wine (I like Chablis)
2 tablespoons chopped fresh parsley
Toast

Melt butter; add scallops, wine, and parsley. Sauté until golden and serve on toast.

Serves 3–4.

Towd Point Bouillabaisse

A friend needled me several summers to make some bouillabaisse. Now, I had enjoyed wonderful bouillabaisse in several fine French restaurants, but I never, never attempted to prepare any. Why? Well, whenever I came across a recipe it was too complicated in every way. I didn't have the time, ingredients, courage, or patience to go through with it.

However, the thought rankled in my mind. I hated to admit defeat. Suddenly one day the light dawned. The French were good cooks because they made the most of what they had on hand. I had on hand the greatest selection of seafood imaginable, so why not give it a try?

I came up with the following recipe which, I think, is one of my best. I would, however, like to suggest that you follow the French idea and use what you can obtain. For instance, we had Towd Point bouillabaisse the other night and I substituted soft-shell clams for hard clams, left out the crab meat, filleted large porgies and added more wine to stretch the dish, and it was better than ever. Take out some of the shells but leave some in for effect. If you're real cagey, you can leave them all in. If you're ravenous and serve nothing else for the meal, this will take care of two.

TOWD POINT BOUILLABAISSE

½ dozen cherrystone clams in shell
½ dozen oysters
½ cup crab meat
1 dozen mussels in shell (optional)
½ pound fillet of flounder
2 tablespoons butter
1 8-ounce can tomato sauce
½ cup water
½ teaspoon Italian seasoning or pinch of basil and bay leaf
Dash Worcestershire sauce
½ cup white wine (if desired)
¼ teaspoon salt
⅛ teaspoon pepper
½ teaspoon paprika

Scrub the shellfish. Cut the flounder in pieces and gently sauté it in the butter. Add everything else and simmer, covered, for 10 minutes. Serve with a slice of French bread on top and more on the side for dunking.

Serves 2–4.

SAVE SOME FOR NEXT SUMMER

Because some of our precious shellfish are disappearing, conservation rules have been adopted for their protection, and you should know about these.

Localities differ, I know, but the regulations of the Town of Southampton are fairly typical.

Hard clams must be one inch thick.

Soft clams or steamers must be two inches long.

Scallops (or escalops) must have one year's growth ring showing. No scallops can be taken from the water between January 1 and September 15.

Crabs must be five inches from point to point (of its shell), and no person shall catch any female crab bearing eggs. These look like sponge sacs hanging on the front of the crab.

Oysters may be taken only in months which have the letter "R" in them and must be three inches long.

So far as I know, there are no conservation rules in the East regarding mussels, but it is very important for you to know that mussels are quarantined along the entire coast of California from May until October. This is because they eat a plankton which is blooming during that time and which, assimilated by the mussels, causes them to poison humans.

Sauces for Shellfish

COCKTAIL SAUCE

1 12-ounce bottle chili sauce
Juice of ½ lemon
¼ cup horseradish
Dash Worcestershire sauce

Blend together. Will keep in refrigerator for quite a while. Use for clams on half shell, cold shrimp, crabs, and oysters on the half shell. It is even good spread on crackers!

It's fun to have this on hand when you come back from an afternoon's digging for clams. While you sort them and clean and open them, have this handy for sneaking some littlenecks.

HOT MELTED BUTTER

Good for dipping crabs, mussels, steamed clams, or oysters.
1 cup butter
2 teaspoons Worcestershire sauce
2 teaspoons prepared mustard
2 tablespoons chili sauce
2 drops Tabasco sauce
4 teaspoons lemon juice
2 teaspoons chopped parsley

Melt butter and add the rest of the seasonings. Heat until bubbly. Makes 1¾ cups.

George, the maître d' at the Beverly Hills Hotel in California, gave me this. He got it from *Sunset* magazine.

TARTARE SAUCE

- 1 cup mayonnaise
- 1 teaspoon finely minced onion
- 1 teaspoon finely minced pickle
- 1 tablespoon capers
- 1 tablespoon tarragon vinegar

Mix everything together and chill well. Makes about 1¼ cups.

GARLIC DIP

- 1 cup melted butter
- 2 crushed cloves garlic
- 1 teaspoon chopped parsley

Melt butter; add garlic and parsley and simmer for a few minutes.

Steamed cherrystones are delicious dunked in this.

VINEGAR SAUCE

(For Oysters)

- ½ cup vinegar
- ½ cup water
- ¼ teaspoon salt
- ⅛ teaspoon pepper
- Dash of Tabasco sauce

Mix vinegar, water, salt, pepper, and Tabasco sauce.

Index

Hook'em
and
Cook'em

For my grandsons
RICHARD BRIGGS DAY and STEWART GARRISON DAY

Contents

Hook'em
and
Cook'em

I LOVE FISH AND FISHING

I love fish and fishing. Ever since I was a little girl, when I dropped my first line in the Sinepuxent Bay behind Ocean City, Maryland, I have been hooked but good. I never fail to thrill when the tiniest nibble sends its message to me or a game fish strikes. Each and every kind of fishing I've done I've loved, and there's a great deal more to do and experience. There aren't really enough hours in the day for me to do all the fishing I want. If I fished all day, every day, I don't think I'd get my fill of either fish or fishing.

It is with humility that I try to tell you how to hook them, because there is always so much more to learn. When I exchange ideas with other fishermen I think I know nothing. However, I've been doing this for years, and since I'm usually lucky, I hope some of my methods will help you to gain this same enthusiasm.

With the exception of a few days of deep-sea fishing in Florida and Mexico, my fishing has been confined to the eastern seaboard waters, especially Peconic Bay, the Shinnecock inlet, Montauk, and Long Island Sound, and I write about the fish caught there. I imagine it would be hard to find better fishing or a better variety anywhere else. So the suggestions I put forth in this little book will be helpful in other places, because bait and ways don't vary too much.

The same goes for the cleaning, preparation, and cooking of fish. The sauces and seasonings that give a fish dish charm here would do the same for a choice catch in Carolina, Florida, or California.

Try both fishing and fish and see if you can't add a joy to your life the same as I have done. In this past year I've had a loss that will be deep and lasting, but fishing with all the beauty, excitement, and concentration that go with it helped give me a peace of mind that nothing else could do.

BUNNY DAY
Towd Point

GADGETS

Any ardent fisherman is a sitting duck in a tackle store. That is where all my money goes. I might do better in a beauty parlor, but I do get a nice tan out of it.

I think the nicest thing a beginner could buy is a little spinning rod and reel. Then he could go to any inlet, harbor, or bay and get a strike and have lots of fun. The next is a light boat rod if he is going to do any fishing from a boat. From there on out he could build up forever. There is no end to it.

But to clean a fish you must have a good *sharp* knife and keep it sharp all the time. The following is a list of many gadgets that will help a great deal.

fish skinner
hook disgorger
fillet knife
shears
killy trap
seine net
white-gas lamp
bait pail
pail
fish scaler
drop nets
fish stringer

killy box
gaff
landing net

P.S. This list was made with the help of my friend Muriel Altenkirch.

P.P.S. Note: You will sometimes find in recipes calling for canned soups that the empty 10½-ounce soup can is further used as a measuring device for milk, cream, or water.

PLAY IT BY EAR

When the wind is in the west the fish bite the best. When the wind is in the east the fish bite the least. Everyone has his own peculiarities, and I am no exception.

I believe that the early worm catches the fish—the earlier, the better. I believe that the fish take a siesta at noonday. I believe when they are really hungry they will take almost any bait. I believe when they are not hungry nothing will coax them. I believe they bite on the outgoing tide because they chase the small bait out. I believe they bite on the incoming tide because they chase the small bait in. I believe they bite again at sunset. Like humans, they like a bedtime snack.

But how come I went out one Sunday at noon at slack tide with just bloodworms and caught eighteen weakfish, the largest kingfish I've ever seen, and a half dozen porgies?

So the best thing to do is to carry several kinds of bait, several-sized hooks, and enough tackle to vary the rigs.

Some people like to anchor a boat and catch the fish on the bottom. Some like to drift or try several spots. Why not try both?

I contend that you have to smell them out. And speaking of smelling, it is true that bluefish schools smell like watermelon. Go to different holes, try several methods, change bait and rigs. If you don't get a bite, go someplace else. If you don't get any bites at all, give up and try some other day. Someday, if you play it by ear, you'll get one.

And I beg of you, do the same with the recipes. Every recipe in this little book is interchangeable. The flavor of the salt pork is just as delectable on porgies as it is on kings or weaks. The almond and grape recipes are just as good on any fillet, and of course the tomato flavor goes with almost anything. Try any of the recipes or sauces with any fish you may catch. You'll be surprised at some wonderful discoveries. So play it by ear anywhere, with anything, and I guarantee you'll soon love fish and fishing.

Most of my recipes are very simple because I believe the taste of fresh fish is so wonderful that it does not need a lot of fancy cooking. A fish doused with butter and broiled is delectable, but the addition of white grapes and a little white wine will make it superb and it is still easy to prepare.

And don't be misled because I use so many local names. I happen to like the sound of them. Try the recipes!

INCOMING TIDE

Around the early part of April when the first false spring comes, I get itchy for the cottage. It isn't that I'm anxious to dig out the winter dirt, but I dream about catching those sweet little flounders.

So in the middle of the month we have the water turned on, the phone and the electricity connected, a fresh gas tank installed—and we are in business.

The drive out is fun. I have gotten into the habit of packing an especially nice picnic basket which includes a bottle of wine and thin crabmeat sandwiches. Usually we delight in pointing out familiar landmarks.

And as we get closer to the salt water we enjoy watching Daisy, a small honey-colored cocker, sniff and bounce around the car because she knows where she is heading.

Even the first musty smell when we unlock the door seems good. We are ready to begin a new summer.

Someone lights a fire in the little iron stove. Someone turns on the oven, and someone plugs in the electric heater. In no time at all we are cozy and warm.

Of course on the way out I stopped and bought blood-worms. So the next day, when I have done enough cleaning to ease my conscience, I pull my spinning rod from its hiding place and take whoever will come with me to my favorite flounder spot. It is a beautiful place about halfway down the dune road toward the Shinnecock inlet. It is all sand, dunes, marshes, and salt water. It is wild with gulls and terns screeching and it fills me with a nameless joy. I am so glad to be back.

Alewives and Shad

Several springs ago, on our opening trip, our curiosity was aroused by a number of people fishing and grabbing and netting something from a creek on the Noyac road.

Upon closer investigation we found that with nets, hands, and scoops they were getting fish with great glee. They told us that they were catching shad, so with our bare hands we joined them because if there's any fish I love, it's shad. In no time we had a lot of fun and a whale of a load of shad.

We brought them home, distributed some among friends who like the fish, and kept some for ourselves.

I carefully baked mine in a slow oven (200°) for several hours, the way you're supposed to cook shad to melt the bones.

Regally I surrounded the dish with decorations and presented it to the family. I can't describe the dry, tasteless, boniest fish I ever ate. It was awful! And it made me nearly die to think that my friends were going through the same torture.

I found out later that the fish were alewives that ran up the stream the same time and the same way the shad do and that people salt them down the way they do herring and they eat them in the winter.

HOW TO COOK ALEWIVES

If you do catch yourself a mess of alewives, this is what you do, according to Frank Marcy.

30 alewives
fat for frying
flour for coating
1½ quarts white vinegar
1½ quarts water
2 tablespoons salt
1 tablespoon sugar
½ teaspoon peppercorns
1 tablespoon pickling spices
3 Bermuda onions, sliced

Clean and scale the fish. Roll them in the flour and fry in the fat for about 10 minutes. Drain. In the meantime make a brine of the remaining ingredients. Put the fish in a large crock in the brine, with sliced onions between the layers. Set in a cool place for a week. Amazingly enough, the bones dissolve and the fish will keep indefinitely.

HOW TO COOK SHAD

But if you are lucky enough to catch shad, here is a recipe that is simply wonderful.

CAROLYN'S BONE-MELTING SHAD

3-pound or better shad
2 quarts water
1 tablespoon vinegar
2 tablespoons lemon juice
1 teaspoon paprika
¼ teaspoon salt
⅛ teaspoon pepper
3 tablespoons butter

Put cleaned shad in a baking pan that can be used on the top of the stove. Pour in the water, add the vinegar, and boil for 15 minutes. Drain the water off thoroughly. Keep the shad in the pan. Add the lemon juice, paprika, salt, pepper, and rub the shad with the butter. Put a tight lid on or cover the pan with heavy foil. Bake at 200° for 6 hours. Remove the cover once or twice and baste. The combination of butter and paprika will give the fish a good color, and the lemon juice and tight cover will keep the fish nice and juicy.

When serving, fold back the top of the fish and remove the remains of the backbone. It will be soft, like the bones of canned salmon. There will be very few bones left, and they will be so soft you will hardly notice them. I really didn't believe this would happen. But I cross my heart and hope to die if it doesn't melt 90 per cent of the bones! Serves 4.

CATHERINE'S SHAD

1 boned and filleted shad
3 tablespoons butter
2 tablespoons lemon juice
½ teaspoon paprika

Melt half of the butter in a baking pan. Place the fillets in it and add the rest of the butter, lemon juice, and the paprika. Broil under a preheated broiler for 10 minutes, basting two or three times to keep the fish nice and moist. This feeds two piggish shad lovers, with fresh spring asparagus and parsley new potatoes on the side.

Flounder and Fluke Fun

In early April and then again in September the little flounder or flat has his day. He is plentiful, fun to catch, and is the sweetest fish to eat.

He has a counterpart that follows him a month or so later, called the fluke. It took me years to tell the difference, but now I think I know. The fluke has a nearly symmetrical mouth, and its gape is very wide. The flounder has a very small mouth, and the eyes and color are usually on the right side. The flounder is usually smaller; however, I caught some that had to be filleted, they were so large.

The fluke is generally large enough to be filleted. There are many devoted people who argue the merits of each fish, but to tell the truth, if you prepared both for me I wouldn't be able to tell the difference. They are a wonderful fish to cook because they are so sweet and white and nice, and they take to a variety of sauces so easily that it is difficult to say which is better. And for just plain pan-fried or broiled for breakfast, it is worth getting up.

HOW TO CATCH FLOUNDER AND FLUKE

I received a little spinning rod for my birthday, and it is the best gift I've ever had. There are many times when I can't go out in the boat and yet I have that terrific urge to catch a fish, so I just grab my little rod and reel and hie me to one of my favorite spots.

You can spin for any small salt-water fish. You cast and reel in, cast and reel in, until you get a strike. Because the rod and tackle are so light, every fish is fun and great sport. Little fish fight and feel like game fish. I love it.

When I fish from the boat for bottom fish, which are what fluke and flounder are, I use a light glass boat rod. That's all you need. On these two rods I've caught every kind of fish Peconic Bay has to offer.

For spinning for flounder, I use a ½- to ¾-ounce sinker and a No. 9 hook. The hook is placed just above but close to the sinker. Use cut bloodworms for bait. On the boat rod I attach a spreader, a 2- to 3-ounce sinker, and a No. 9 at each end of the spreader.

For fluke, use a No. 4 or 5 hook and a round type of sinker heavy enough to hold on the bottom. Place the leader and hook six inches above the sinker; and a second hook can be tied to the line about two feet above this. For bait, fluke prefer a live killy or shiner.

Now I really will let you in on a secret! In April my son Joel and I went to Shinnecock Bay for flounder or fluke. It so happened the flounders were running. I had bought a new spreader with a chum trap attached to the middle (an elongated metal container with holes). In this trap we stuffed crushed mussels, shell and all.

Joel placed the two hooks on each side of the spreader and baited both with worms. In very little time there was action. We caught fish as fast as we could hit the bottom. We almost always had two on at once and several times three! We had a dozen bloodworms with us, so when they were gone we gave up and had forty nice fat flounders.

HOW TO CLEAN FLOUNDER AND FLUKE

The most important thing about cleaning fish is to do it as soon as possible. Entrails in and scales on lessen the good freshness of the fish. Some people I know gut their fish while they are still out fishing. I like to bring the boat in, gather my tools, and clean them at the water's edge. No matter what, it is a messy, smelly job, so why dirty up the kitchen? Besides, the head and innards dumped in the water attract more bait and crabs.

You need a cutting board, scissors, a sharp knife, a fish scaler, and a pair of working gloves. These are the basic implements for cleaning all fish.

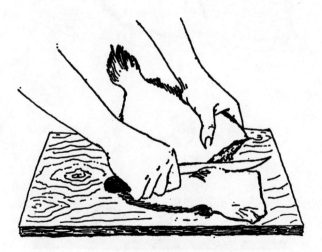

Place the fish (flounder or fluke) on the board. Grasp the fish firmly with your left hand, and that's why I wear gloves. These fish are very slippery.

Cut the head off behind the gills, following the line of the head. Then slit under the belly from an apparent small hole toward where the head used to be. Scrape out the innards.

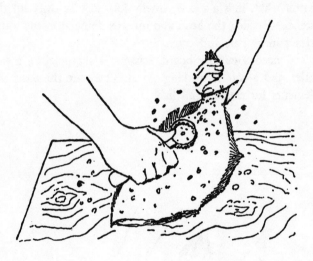

To remove the scales, grasp the tail firmly and, using the scaler, scrape forward from the tail. The underside is smooth because these fish lie on their bellies.

Wash well. If they are small fish they are ready for frying, broiling, or baking—or any way that does not call for fillets.

HOW TO FILLET FLOUNDER AND FLUKE

Remove the head and entrails from the fish. Then place the fish flat on the cutting board. With a very sharp knife—and you can buy a good fillet knife—cut along the backbone from the head to the tail. Run the knife under the flesh along the bone toward the fin. Lift the fillet out and repeat for the remaining three sides. You get four nice fillets from each fish.

To skin a fillet, place it on the board with the small end toward you. Work the knife under the piece until you can hold it tightly with your left hand. When you obtain a firm

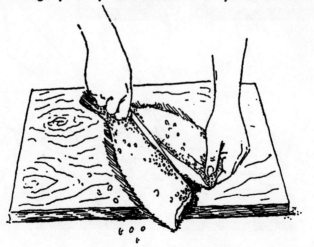

grip, work the knife smoothly to the end. The skin will separate from the flesh and you will be delighted with the result.

This takes a little practice, but it is worth the effort. There
are so many charming things to do with fillets, and besides,
you may have a crank who refuses to eat any fish with bones.

Invest your money in a good knife or you will be wasting
your time.

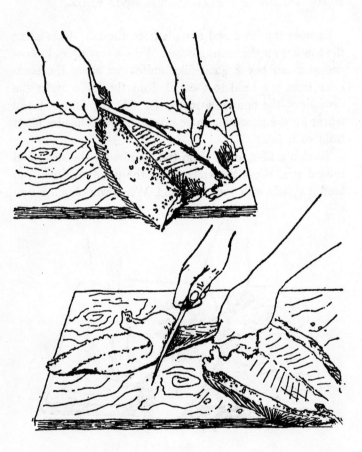

HOW TO EAT 'EM

How many times have you heard people say, "I don't like fish except a fillet?" I think it's a sin and a crime to condemn a fish just because the poor thing has *bones*. I've been watching my friends lately and I've come to the conclusion that most people don't know how to eat fish properly. A fish beautifully prepared can be ruined by jabbing in a fork and coming out with a mess of flesh, skin, and bones. Haven't you seen people do this? They put it in their mouths and surreptitiously spit out the bones, in the meantime trying to say, "This is good," but leaving a plateful of fish behind and a desire never to touch fish again.

So I think an explanation of how to eat fish is in order.

To eat flounder, cut along the backbone from the head to the tail. Ease the knife between the flesh and the bone, working toward the fin. Lay back the meat. Repeat on the other side. Lift out the backbone and cut out the little bones on the side. *Voilà*.

Any other crisply fried fish is handled this way. With a knife, loosen the flesh from the split side from the head to the tail. Gently fold the top piece over so that both sides of the fish are spread out on the plate. If the flesh is nice and white and well done, it will do this easily. Now you have the fish lying flat. With a fork, loosen and remove the backbone. (It's a good idea to have a bone dish on the side.) Then with a knife cut down the side with the little bones and lift them out. Your remaining fish should be as boneless as any fillet and ready to eat plain or with a fine sauce.

A broiled fish that still has the bone in should be laid out flat so that all you have to do is lift out the backbone and cut the fine bones from the side.

A small baked fish is boned in the same manner.

A large baked fish that is sliced crosswise is prepared in this manner. Fold the top half back, remove the large backbone, lay back again, and slice through. With the little care and the little time it takes, the proper eating will make your fish that much more enjoyable. And before long you'll find that you'll like all the good fish in the sea.

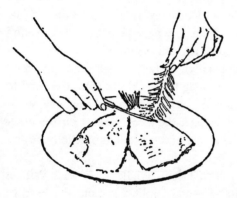

HOW TO COOK FLOUNDER AND FLUKE

ALMOND FILLETS

8 fillets (almost any kind)
1 cup peeled, slivered almonds
½ cup butter
¼ teaspoon salt

Have half of the butter sizzling in the broiler pan. Add the fillets, almonds, salt, and the rest of the butter. Broil for 8 to 10 minutes. Serves 4.

BAKED CHEESE FILLETS

1 pound fillets
1 10½-ounce can cheese soup
¼ cup milk
2 tablespoons chili sauce
dash Worcestershire sauce

Place fish in buttered baking dish. Mix the soup with milk, chili sauce, and Worcestershire. Cover the fish with the mixture. Bake at 350° for 30 minutes. Serves 2 to 4.

ELEANOR'S FLOUNDER FILLETS

2 nice-sized fillets
4 tablespoons butter

Bring half of the butter to the sizzling point in an old pie tin. Remove from the heat. Place the fillets in this and put the rest of the butter on the top. Broil for about 8 to 10 minutes. This little trick will keep the fish moist inside and crisp and brown on both the top and the bottom. Serves 2.

FLOUNDERS FLANAGAN

4 flounders, cleaned
⅛ pound butter
½ teaspoon Worcestershire sauce
⅛ teaspoon celery salt
4 bay leaves
¼ teaspoon seasoned salt
⅛ teaspoon pepper
½ cup grated Parmesan cheese

Melt the butter; add the rest of the ingredients. Pour half of this mixture into the bottom of a broiling pan while the mixture is hot. Add the flounders and pour the rest of the mixture over them. Broil, without turning, for 8 to 10 minutes. This is an excellent way to cook a big mess of flounders for a big mess of people. Just increase fish, sauce, and people.

FORT POND FILLETS

8 fillets of flounder
¼ cup seasoned bread crumbs
½ cup butter
½ onion, thinly sliced
½ cup thinly sliced mushrooms
¼ teaspoon salt
⅛ teaspoon black pepper

Roll the fillets in the seasoned bread crumbs. Melt the butter in a pan and sauté the onion slices and mushrooms until the onions are transparent. Add the fillets, salt, and pepper and sauté for 10 minutes, turning once. Add more butter if necessary. Serves 4.

FILLET OF FLOUNDER IN SOUR CREAM QUOGUE

4 flounder fillets
¼ teaspoon salt
⅛ teaspoon pepper
1 teaspoon lemon juice
1 cup sour cream

Lay flounder fillets in buttered baking dish. Sprinkle with salt, pepper, and lemon juice. Cover with sour cream. Bake 20 to 25 minutes in a hot oven, 400°. Serves 2 to 4.

FLYING POINT FILLETS

8 fillets of flounder or fluke
½ cup mayonnaise
½ cup fine seasoned bread crumbs

Spread the fillets with the mayonnaise and roll them in the seasoned bread crumbs. Arrange them in a hand grill and charcoal-broil over a fire for 4 to 5 minutes on each side. Serves 4.

HAMPTON POACHED FILLETS

6 medium fillets
3 tablespoons butter
½ medium onion, chopped
2 tablespoons chopped parsley
¼ teaspoon salt
⅛ teaspoon pepper
¼ teaspoon thyme
½ cup white wine
¼ cup water

Melt butter in a skillet. Add the onion, parsley, and fish fillets. Season with the salt, pepper, and thyme. Pour the wine and water over the fish and poach gently for 10 to 15 minutes, depending on the thickness of the fillets. Good served nice and hot right from the skillet. Serves 4 to 6.

GIN LANE FLOUNDER

8 fillets of flounder or fluke
½ cup mayonnaise
1 tablespoon lemon juice
½ cup sliced olives

Arrange the fillets in a broiling pan. Spread them with mayonnaise. Sprinkle with lemon juice and sliced olives. Broil for 10 to 12 minutes. Serves 4.

JEAN'S OVEN-FRIED FISH FILLETS

12 small flounder fillets
2 tablespoons prepared mustard
¼ cup bread crumbs
¼ teaspoon salt
⅛ teaspoon pepper
¼ teaspoon thyme
¼ teaspoon orégano
2 tablespoons salad oil
½ teaspoon paprika

Heat oven to 500°. Grease or line a flat baking dish with foil. Brush both sides of the fillets with mustard. Place on baking pan. Combine bread crumbs and dry ingredients and spread on each fish. Sprinkle each fillet with the salad oil and paprika. *Bake 10 minutes only.* Serves 4. Please try this one. It is *so* delicious and *so* easy.

MIDGE'S FISH FILLETS

1 pound fish fillets (This does things for halibut.)
½ cup white wine
1 tablespoon butter
1 tablespoon flour
3 tablespoons sour cream
2 tablespoons capers

Place fish in a buttered pan and pour the wine over them. Bake at 400° for 25 to 30 minutes, depending on the thickness. Remove to a hot platter. Make a roux of the flour and butter and add to the drippings in the pan in which the fish had been cooked. Stir well and add the sour cream and capers. Simmer until blended and heated. Pour this sauce over the fish and serve immediately. Serves 2.

RUTH'S TOMATO FILLETS

8 fillets
1 10½-ounce can tomato soup
½ 10½-ounce can water
¼ teaspoon basil
½ teaspoon sugar
¼ teaspoon salt
⅛ teaspoon pepper

Place the fillets in a buttered or foil-lined baking pan. Add the soup mixed with water and season with basil, sugar, salt, and pepper. Bake at 375° for about 25 minutes. Serves 4 to 6.

SHINNECOCK FLOUNDER OR FLUKE

4 flounders or flukes
¼ pound salt pork, sliced
½ cup cracker crumbs
⅛ teaspoon salt
⅛ teaspoon pepper

Gash each fish twice on the top and insert slices of salt pork in the gashes. Fry remaining slices of salt pork in a baking pan. Place the fish in the hot fat. Sprinkle with cracker crumbs, salt, and pepper. Bake at 400° for ½ hour. Very special with tomato or mustard sauce. Serves 4.

CALLA'S DIET RECIPE
FOR FILLETS

1 pound fillet of flounder or any other nice fillet
½ 8-ounce can consommé

Spread fillets on a broiling pan lined with foil. Pour the consommé on top and broil for 15 minutes. Serves 2 to 3.

WAINSCOTT FLOUNDER

4 flounders
¼ pound salt pork, diced
½ cup corn meal

Fry salt pork until crisp. Remove from pan and keep hot. Roll the flounders in the corn meal and fry in the hot salt-pork fat, turning once after about 5 to 6 minutes. Serve with the hot salt pork. Serves 4.

WATERMILL FILLETS

8 fillets
½ cup butter
1 cup white seedless grapes
¼ cup white wine

Have half of the butter sizzling in the broiling pan. Put the
fillets in the hot butter. Add the grapes and white wine and
broil until nice and brown on top, about 8 to 12 minutes.
Serves 4.

BREAKFAST FILLETS OR
FRIED FLOUNDERS

8 fillets or small whole flounders
½ cup flour or seasoned bread crumbs
¼ teaspoon salt
⅛ teaspoon pepper
bacon fat for frying

Put flour or seasoned bread crumbs, salt, and pepper in a
paper sack. Shake the fish in this until well coated. In
the meantime have fat heating in the pan. When the fat is
good and hot, put in the fish and fry for 10 minutes, turning
once. There's nothing like an old-fashioned cast-iron frying
pan for creating crispness.

Thar She Blows

Call them blowfish, bottlefish, sea squab, or chicken of the sea, but don't throw them back into the water when you catch them.

Years ago when we cruised we were bothered when we fished by silly little fish that took our bait. When we took them off the hook we amused the children by tickling the bellies of these fish because they blew themselves up and became funny round balls. When everyone tired of their antics they were thrown back into the sea.

I can't remember who told me they were good to eat or when or how I learned to clean them, but I have been grateful ever since. Cleaned properly, they become a solid chunk of firm white flesh that is easily prepared and delicious to eat. They lend themselves nicely to a variety of seasonings and flavorings. For instance, I had a guest for dinner who declared she'd never eat or like any kind of fish. I cooked blowfish the way the French cook frogs' legs, called them frogs' legs, and after my guest raved and ate all she could hold I confessed she'd eaten and enjoyed *fish*.

HOW TO CATCH BLOWFISH

One Sunday we went to my favorite weakfish hole, on Little Peconic Bay, facing Rose's Grove. However, the wind was blowing hard, the weather was threatening, and the weaks were not biting, so we moved behind Holmes Hill, a beautiful high sand cliff facing Robins Island, to catch a few blows.

Blowfish swim in very shallow water. I have felt them around my legs just a few yards from shore. I've caught them in as little as three or four feet of water.

They have a tiny mouth that sucks the bait, so I suggest that you use your lightest tackle and your smallest hooks. Use a 1- or 2-ounce sinker, two of the smallest flounder hooks, one above the other. Slice squid into the tiniest pieces and bait the hooks. The fish are so small and so smart that frequently they will steal your bait without your feeling anything, so check your line often. They are fun to catch, because they keep you alert and the eating will be your reward.

HOW TO CLEAN BLOWFISH

The skin of the blowfish is very tough and prickly, so I heartily recommend that you wear gloves when handling them. I usually like to work without gloves, but I found my hands have a funny itching for a while after handling blowfish.

Place the fish on a board, underside down. With a good knife, cut right through the fish, directly behind the head or eyes to the bottom skin. Grab the skin and peel it off the way you would a glove. The innards will fall out and you will work free a solid piece of fish flesh that does faintly resemble a frog's leg. It will take a little pulling and tugging, but after you get the knack of it, it will become simple, and I guarantee you will love the taste of blowfish.

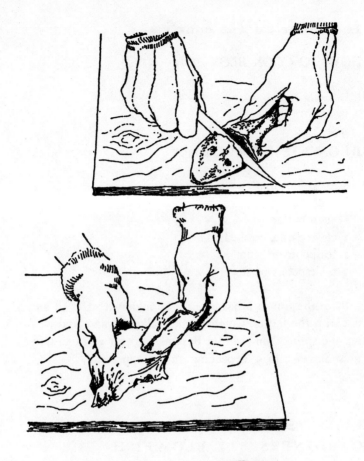

HOW TO COOK BLOWFISH

BLOWFISH ORÉGANO

8 to 10 blowfish
¼ cup olive oil
¼ cup butter
1 clove garlic, crushed
1 teaspoon orégano
3 tablespoons parsley

Place the fish in a baking pan. Sprinkle with the oil and dot with the butter. Combine the garlic, orégano, and parsley and sprinkle on the fish. Bake at 375° for 25 to 30 minutes. Serves 3 to 5, depending on the appetites.

GARDINERS BAY BLOWFISH

6 blowfish
½ cup flour
1 teaspoon seasoned salt
fat for frying (I prefer bacon fat.)

Mix the flour with the seasoned salt. Roll the blowfish in this or put flour, salt, and fish in a paper bag and shake until well coated. In the meantime heat fat to 350°. Fry blowfish about 4 minutes on each side. Serves 2 to 3.

BLOWFISH PROVENÇAL

10 blowfish
¼ pound butter
2 tablespoons chopped parsley
2 cloves garlic, crushed
¼ teaspoon salt
⅛ teaspoon pepper

Melt the butter; add the parsley, garlic, and blowfish. Sprinkle with the salt and pepper. Sauté the blowfish for 4 to 5 minutes on one side. Turn. Sauté 4 to 5 minutes on the other. In other words, have them reach a nice golden tan. Serve these with French bread and white wine. Serves 4.

RIVERHEAD BLOWFISH

12 blowfish
½ cup butter
¼ teaspoon salt
⅛ teaspoon pepper
½ cup sherry

Sauté the fish in the butter until golden. Sprinkle with the salt and pepper. At the last minute add the sherry. Serves 4 to 6.

PECONIC BAY BLOWFISH

8 to 10 blowfish
¼ cup olive oil
½ cup Chablis or other white wine
1 teaspoon rosemary
¼ teaspoon salt
⅛ teaspoon black pepper

Arrange the fish in a baking dish. Pour on the oil and the wine and sprinkle with the seasonings. Bake at 425° for 25 minutes. Serves 4.

RIVIERA BLOWFISH

12 blowfish
1 package Italian-style spaghetti sauce mix
1 8-ounce can tomato sauce
½ cup red wine
2 tablespoons Parmesan cheese

Arrange the blowfish in a baking dish. Prepare the sauce mix according to the directions on the package, using tomato sauce and substituting the red wine for half of the water. Stir until mixed, without cooking, and pour over the fish. Bake at 400° for 25 to 30 minutes. Add the cheese after you remove the fish from the oven. Serves 4 to 6.

NEW SUFFOLK BLOWFISH

10 blowfish
½ cup seasoned bread crumbs
oil for frying

Roll blowfish in the seasoned crumbs and fry in the oil for 6 minutes on each side. Serve with lemon and a mustard sauce. Serves 4.

SHELTER ISLAND BLOWFISH

8 blowfish
¼ pound butter
¼ teaspoon salt
⅛ teaspoon pepper

Melt the butter in a pan. Add the blowfish. Sprinkle with the salt and pepper. Sauté for 4 to 5 minutes. Turn. Sauté 4 to 5 minutes more. Serves 3 to 4.

SOUTHOLD BROILED BLOWFISH

8 to 10 blowfish
½ cup melted butter or salad oil
1 teaspoon fish seasoning
¼ teaspoon Worcestershire sauce
1 tablespoon lemon juice

Arrange blowfish in a foil-lined broiling pan. Combine the melted butter or oil, fish seasoning, Worcestershire sauce, and lemon juice. Broil for 10 to 12 minutes, basting once. Serves 4.

Porgies

THE SAFARI

Funny how some things become traditional. Before we had become aware of it, the gang next door and our family started an annual safari.

Early in the morning when the mood hit us we collected every available boat, fishing tackle, bait, and person and headed for the red buoy near Nassau Point. Some of our boats were better and faster than others, so we hitched the strong with the weak and rode out to sea looking like a crazy regatta. At a certain point a halt was called and anchors were cast. We all stayed hitched together so no one could miss what was caught or, more important, what was said. The bantering back and forth and the kidding were an important part of the safari.

Every year we have been lucky. We have always filled the boat with porgies and a few other varieties of fish—so much so that when a bushel basket was filled we called a halt because that was all we wanted to clean and eat.

In the afternoon we sent the men to dig cherrystones and littleneck clams while we women prepared and planned the evening picnic. We wrapped porgies in foil with sliced onions and potatoes. We soaked corn in the husks in salt water, we made cocktail sauce, sliced lemons, produced bowls of cucumbers and tomatoes, and stashed the paper plates, cups, napkins, and fire-building equipment in baskets.

When the sun started to lower we put everything in the boats, tied them together again, and headed for Holmes Hill. On this high sand cliff facing the Peconic and overlooking Robins Island and the North Fork, we can survey the two Peconics, Shelter Island, and the Shinnecock on a clear day. It is a magnificent spot.

We had clams on the half shell with our cocktails, followed by clams roasted on the coals, porgies cooked in foil, corn roasted in the husks, salad, pickles, watermelon, and coffee.

As the cat died down (meaning the fire) we sat around and sang and told stories and reminisced.

It was always a delightful day and evening, one never to be forgotten.

HOW TO CATCH PORGIES

Porgies are the easiest to catch in the bay because they are the most abundant. The first hundred are good; after that you can't give them away, especially uncleaned.

Porgies are a bottom fish and they run from half a pound to three or four pounds in deep water.

Use a light tackle—a nice boat rod—and rig two hooks 2/o one above the other with a two-ounce sinker, depending on the current. Their favorite bait is squid, but when they are really hungry they might take clams and worms or most anything you happen to have aboard. Some people like to use a real small hook 3-12. Don't let these numbers confuse you; any tackle store will help you out. I have heard this rig called a Peconic rig, but recently I heard someone call it a Hollywood rig!

Let your line out until it rests easily on the bottom. Pull as soon as you get a bite. You don't usually lose porgies because they grab the hook, then of course they are hooked. Besides, they don't have much fight. But don't let that stop you—a fresh porgy is good to eat.

HOW TO CLEAN PORGIES

I like to scale the porgy first because they are mean to do. Grasp the fish firmly by the tail, and with a scaler or knife scrape from tail to head, holding it away from you. Do this outside near the water if you possibly can because porgy scales are large and tough and fly all around. Next cut off the head, slit the underside, and scrape out the innards. Wash and ice, and you will have something nice!

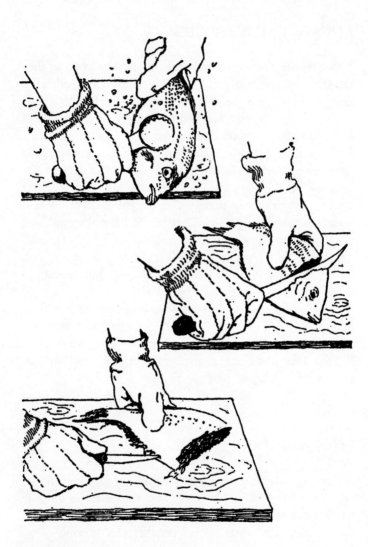

HOW TO COOK PORGIES

BROILED PORGIES

    4 1-pound porgies
    4 tablespoons melted butter
    4 tablespoons lemon juice
    4 tablespoons catsup
    1 teaspoon seafood seasoning

Broil the porgies 8 to 10 minutes on each side, basting with a mixture made of the rest of the ingredients. Serves 4.

HOLMES HILL PORGIES

    12 porgies
    12 thin slices onion
    12 thin slices lemon
    12 thin slices tomatoes
    12 slices bacon
    12 squares of foil sized to wrap each fish

Place each porgy on the foil. Arrange the rest of the ingredients in order on top of each porgy. Wrap tightly and cook over a charcoal fire for about 45 minutes. Serves 12.

CREOLE PORGIES

4 porgies
½ green pepper, minced
3 tablespoons olive oil
½ onion, minced
1 pound can tomatoes
1 teaspoon sugar
¼ teaspoon salt
⅛ teaspoon pepper
¼ teaspoon thyme
1 crushed garlic bud

Cook the onion and pepper in the olive oil until soft. Add the tomatoes, sugar, salt, pepper, thyme, and garlic. In the meantime place the porgies in a buttered or foil-lined baking dish. Pour the sauce over the porgies and bake at 400° for 25 to 30 minutes. Serves 4.

STELLA'S PORGIES WITH DILL

4 medium-sized porgies
4 tablespoons butter
4 tablespoons fresh dill, chopped
flour or corn meal for coating
¼ teaspoon salt
⅛ teaspoon pepper

Melt the butter in a saucepan. Add the dill. Roll the fish in the flour seasoned with salt and pepper and sauté in the dill butter until brown, about 8 to 10 minutes on each side. Serves 4.

LITTLE PECONIC PORGIES

6 porgies
1 cup evaporated milk
1 cup flour or fine bread crumbs
½ teaspoon fish seasoning
fat for frying

Roll the porgies in the evaporated milk. Then coat them with the flour or crumbs that have been mixed with the fish seasoning. Fry in hot fat 8 to 10 minutes on each side, depending on the size. This coating will make the skin more delicious than ever. Serves 4 to 6.

PECONIC GRILLED PORGIES

4 medium-sized porgies
4 tablespoons melted butter or salad dressing
4 tablespoons lemon juice
2 teaspoons seasoned salt

Clean the porgies and split them for broiling. Place them in a hand grill. Brush the skin side with the melted butter or salad dressing. Turn and brush on the rest of the butter or dressing, the lemon juice and seasoned salt. This, of course, will be the flesh side. On nice red coals place the grill with the porgies *skin side down*. Broil for 10 minutes. Turn; broil for 10 minutes more. You won't recognize the common porgy—it will be so good! Serves 4.

OVEN-FRIED PORGIES

12 porgies
12 tablespoons salad dressing

Arrange porgies in a foil-lined baking pan. Rub each porgy with the salad dressing and bake at 400° for 25 to 30 minutes. This is the easy way to cook fish for a crowd. Serves 12.

PAN-FRIED PORGIES

4 porgies
½ cup flour or corn meal
¼ teaspoon salt
bacon fat for frying
lemon wedges

Roll the fish in the flour or corn meal or shake them in a paper bag. Fry in hot fat 6 to 8 minutes on each side. Be sure they are nice and crisp and brown on the outside and white and flaky on the inside. Serve with lemon wedges. We love these for breakfast with pan-fried potatoes and heaps of hot coffee. Serves 4.

SEBONAC PORGIES

4 porgies
4 tablespoons fish sauce
4 tablespoons mayonnaise

Mix the fish sauce and the mayonnaise. Spread the mixture on both sides of the cleaned fish. Place in a hand grill, cook over coals for about 8 minutes on each side. Serves 4.

Bluefish

A wild, joyous spot is the rip between Little Peconic and Great Peconic bays just off Robins Island.

My first trip through this rip was about ten years ago, when we had *Day Dream* and were on our first cruise. It was a strange and rough spot and we went through cautiously.

Now almost every night in July, just before sunset and during the afterglow, we troll through these churning waters on the prowl for bluefish. For at twilight the terns start working, the skiffs race out, and the fun begins.

These blues weigh from one to three pounds, perhaps a little more. They are scrappy, gamey, and exciting to catch. I caught my first blue here and was so thrilled I think you could have heard me in New York.

Not only do these blues provide fishing fun, but they are truly marvelous to eat. The deep firm white meat has an excellent flavor and a quality that is unsurpassed. Each summer when I catch and eat my first blue I always say I think it is the best fish, but then I have been known to say that about my first kingfish or weakfish of the season.

But a real thrill in my life was October a year ago when my son sprang a bluefish party off Montauk for my birthday. I caught two ten-pounders and I haven't stopped talking about it, nor dreaming and hoping that I'll do the same thing again.

I froze one of those large blues and we had a dinner party and enjoyed it the night before our trip to California on January 5, 1960. The beauty of the fish and its wonderful flavor brought back the happy, salty memories of the summer.

HOW TO CATCH BLUEFISH

Trolling

Troll at a medium speed. Use a light boat rod with a 2/o reel, 30-pound test line, 3/o to 5/o hook, steel leader (because they will bite off a regular line). Many people use 50 to 75 yards of steel line for weight.

You can use a feather, spoon, block-tin squid, or eel skins. A trick is to use a strip of pork rind with a hook in it. All these things can be bought in a tackle shop.

If the fish are working on top, then no weights are needed. If they are down, add trolling weights from 1½ to 3 ounces, depending on conditions, speed currents, and so forth. Also, to get a line down 30 to 40 feet, a planer may be used if you are off shore.

These babies strike hard and do a lot of fancy jumping and diving, so give them *no* slack and keep them coming as fast as you can.

Blues are found in the surf, inlets, and are especially fond of rough rips. They are capricious fish, and you can sometimes spot them going after live bait and they will refuse to touch yours. They are voracious killers and eat constantly. Terns are good bluefish spotters. Be on the lookout for a working flock. But no matter what, keep going after them, because they can give you the greatest fight and the greatest eating.

HOW TO COOK BLUEFISH

BROILED BLUES

1- to 2-pound bluefish
4 tablespoons garlic spread
2 tablespoons lemon juice
½ teaspoon fish seasoning

Clean and split fish for broiling and remove the large bone
and side bones. Place in a broiling pan. Spread softened
garlic spread on the fish. Sprinkle with the lemon juice and
fish seasoning. Broil 14 to 18 minutes. Fork-test for flakiness.
Serves 2 to 4.

BLUEFISH RIVERHEAD

2 pounds bluefish fillets
1½ cups sour cream
½ cup mayonnaise
2 tablespoons chopped chives
⅛ cup lemon juice
¼ teaspoon salt
⅛ teaspoon pepper

Place the fillets in a buttered baking dish. Mix sour cream,
mayonnaise, chives, lemon juice, salt, and pepper together.
Spread mixture over fish. Bake at 375° for 30 minutes.
Serves 4.

BAKED BLUEFISH

8- to 10-pound bluefish
2 cups stuffing
½ teaspoon salt
⅛ teaspoon pepper
2 tablespoons lemon juice
4 strips bacon

Clean the fish. Leave the head on. Put the stuffing in the cavity which has been sprinkled with salt. Place in a large baking pan lined with foil. Sprinkle the top of the fish with salt, pepper, and lemon juice. Place the strips of bacon across the top. Bake at 400° for 1 hour. Serve on a fish platter and decorate with lemon wedges and parsley. Serves about 6. Salt-pork strips instead of bacon would also be delicious.

BLUEFISH STUFFING

2 cups seasoned poultry stuffing
2 tablespoons minced onion
2 tablespoons minced parsley
2 tablespoons bacon fat
½ teaspoon salt
¼ teaspoon pepper
4 tablespoons water

Brown the onion, celery, and parsley in the bacon fat. Add the salt, pepper, stuffing, and water and mix well. This stuffing can be used for any kind of large fish that you want to bake.

BLUEFISH À LA BARRIDA

8 to 10 bluefish fillets
1 pint olive oil
6 egg yolks
6 cloves garlic (ground in a mortar with 1 teaspoon salt)
2 tablespoons vinegar
1 teaspoon dry mustard

Whip the olive oil, adding the egg yolks and everything else gradually. Spread the bluefish fillets with the homemade mayonnaise and broil until slightly crusty and brown.

This recipe is from fishermen Sarah and Bill Lewis. It must be done with this mayonnaise recipe, because the number of egg yolks is what makes it extra-special.

INLET BLUEFISH

1 bluefish, about 2 pounds
½ cup melted butter
4 tablespoons lemon juice
½ teaspoon onion juice
1 teaspoon A.1. sauce
¼ teaspoon salt
⅛ teaspoon pepper

Split the fish and remove the backbone. Place skin side down and spread open in a buttered or foil-lined pan. Melt the butter and add the lemon juice, onion juice, A.1. sauce, salt, and pepper. Bake at 400° for about ½ hour, basting every so often. Serves 4.

JESSUP NECK BLUEFISH

2 pounds bluefish fillets
1 tablespoon butter
1 tablespoon flour
1 10½-ounce can cream of chicken soup
1 cup light cream
4 tablespoons lemon juice
¼ teaspoon salt
⅛ teaspoon pepper

Place the bluefish fillets in a baking pan. Melt the butter in a saucepan and blend in the flour. Add the chicken soup and cream gradually. Stir constantly, adding the lemon juice, salt, and pepper. Pour over the fish. Bake at 375° for about 25 to 30 minutes. Serves 4.

PLUM GUT BLUEFISH

1 large bluefish
2 cups fine, seasoned bread crumbs
¼ cup olive oil
½ teaspoon orégano
1 pound can tomatoes
1 teaspoon sugar

Clean the fish. Place in a large baking pan that has been lined with foil. Mix the bread crumbs with the olive oil and orégano and spread on the fish. Pour the tomatoes over all and sprinkle with the sugar. Bake at 400° for 1 hour. Test with fork. If meat is white and flaky, it is ready. Serves 4 to 6, depending on size.

POACHED BLUEFISH

1 bluefish, 3 to 5 pounds
1 onion, sliced thin
1 tomato, sliced thin
½ cup dry white wine
½ teaspoon thyme
⅛ teaspoon pepper
¼ teaspoon salt
½ cup sour cream

Layer the onions, tomatoes, and the bluefish in an oblong baking pan. Add the wine, herb, and seasonings. Cover the pan with foil. Bake at 400° for 45 to 50 minutes. Remove the foil and the fish. Stir the sour cream in the pan drippings. Serve in a hot platter with the drippings poured over the fish. Serves 8.

SOUTHAMPTON BLUEFISH

2 pounds bluefish fillets
1 10½-ounce can mushroom soup
½ 10½-ounce can milk
4 tablespoons Parmesan cheese
¼ teaspoon salt
⅛ teaspoon pepper
½ cup seasoned stuffing

Place the fillets in a buttered casserole. Mix the soup and the milk and pour over the fish. Sprinkle with the cheese, salt, pepper, and stuffing. Bake at 400° for ½ hour. Serves 4.

HOW TO CATCH SNAPPERS

On a beautiful late August or September day, suddenly you hear the cry, "The snappers are running." Drop everything and run to the nearest harbor, bay, or inlet with your bamboo pole or spinning rod and you will have the time of your life.

These little blues are tremendous fun to catch, and a pan of them fried in butter is heavenly eating.

You can use a simple bamboo pole with no reel. Use a long-shank snapper hook (Nos. 3 or 4, long shank). Live shiners or spearing is the best bait. Attach a cork float so that the hook is about two to three feet under the water. At the first faint nibble, swing the line in, as these little monkeys get off *fast*.

It is exciting to catch snappers on a spinning rod also. Use tiny lures with or without bait. You should experiment to find which little spoon or lure they like the best. I've had my best luck with double long-shank hooks and live bait, although I have several shiny spoons they just love! Along about the end of September and the first of October snappers get to be almost a pound. I have a real passion for catching these things.

HOW TO COOK SNAPPERS

BRUNCH SNAPPERS

12 snappers, at least
½ cup flour
½ teaspoon seasoned salt
fat for frying

Put the flour, seasoned salt, and snappers in a paper bag. Shake until well coated. Fry in hot fat until brown and crisp, turning once. It takes about 5 to 8 minutes for each side, no more. Serve these with hash-browned potatoes and hot biscuits and nobody will leave your house! Serves 4.

MIDDLE POND SNAPPERS

12 snappers
1 cup evaporated milk
1 cup fine, seasoned bread crumbs
fat for frying

Dip the snappers in the evaporated milk, then in the bread crumbs, or shake them in a bag with the crumbs. Fry at 350° about 4 to 5 minutes on each side. Serves 4 if you *love* snappers, which most people do!

SNAPPERS WITH ALMONDS

6 snappers
¼ cup oil
¼ cup butter
¼ teaspoon salt
⅛ teaspoon pepper
½ cup medium cream
½ cup browned almonds

Brown the snappers in the oil and the butter. Sprinkle with salt and pepper. Remove the snappers and add the cream to the pan and stir. Pour over the snappers and top with the almonds. One person can eat at least two snappers.

WEST NECK SNAPPERS

12 snappers
½ cup butter
½ onion, minced
2 tablespoons minced parsley

Heat the butter until it bubbles; add the minced onion and snappers. Sauté until tan, about 5 to 8 minutes on each side, turning once. Add the chopped parsley when you turn them. Serve on a warm platter with the pan sauce poured on the fish, and lemon slices. Serves 4 to 5.

MIKE McCARTHY'S SNAPPER BLUES

4 ½- to 1-pound snappers
½ pound butter
1 onion, minced very fine
½ pound mushrooms, sliced very thin
2 tablespoons lemon juice
4 squares foil for wrapping

Clean the fish and slit the cavity from head to tail. Sauté the onion in half of the butter until transparent. Add the mushrooms and cook for 1 minute. Place each fish on a square of foil and fill the cavity with the onion and mushroom mixture, dividing it all evenly and letting it spill out of the cavity if necessary. Dot with the remaining butter and sprinkle with lemon juice. Wrap tightly and bake over red coals in charcoal grill for 20 to 25 minutes. Fork-test for flakiness. Serves 4.

Kingfish

My earliest memory is my grandfather standing in the surf at Ocean City, Maryland. Almost every morning he fished for our breakfast. We had to be at the table at eight o'clock every morning, and sometimes it was a hardship. But when we caught a glimpse of a heaped platter of golden fried fish flanked by golden fried potatoes and corn bread, we sat ourselves down in front of a golden cantaloupe with sheer delightful anticipation.

I still think one of the world's most wonderful treats is to have fresh fried fish for breakfast. We often have them at the cottage on Sunday mornings and sometimes even go to the trouble to cart everything to the beach and fry them there. That is really heavenly.

One morning during the first summer at the cottage a neighbor invited me to go fishing for kingfish. I was very pleased because that was the fish my grandfather caught for our breakfast and I was fond of them, and so far I had caught only porgies in the bay. But my friend knew a hole where the kingfish hung out, and sure enough, after several tries I hooked one. I admit I was a bit overenthusiastic, but by golly it was the same fish that my grandfather loved to catch. We caught quite a mess of them, and the next morning we had them for breakfast with cantaloupe, corn bread, and fried potatoes—all of which gave me nostalgia because it tasted just the same and just as good as when I was a little girl.

Many years ago when I was deep-sea fishing off Palm Beach with my son Peter, who was five at the time, I hooked a large kingfish. I almost had him boated when a porpoise jumped out of the water and swallowed the fish, tackle and all. Peter yelled, "My mother caught a whale!" But I won't dare tell you what the captain yelled or how I felt about losing the fish.

HOW TO CATCH KINGFISH

Kingfish play just up from the bottom of deep holes. They also like rips and inlets. Their favorite bait is bloodworms if you are bottom-fishing for them. When they are truly hungry they might nibble at squid, clams, or shrimp. As I said before, my grandfather went surf-casting for them, but that is out of my sphere (next year!). However, I have caught many snapper-sized ones at inlets with my little spinning rod on feathers and spoons and shiners when I have been fishing for snappers. You can also catch them drifting.

For bottom-fishing or drifting, use a light boat rod with 1/o–3/o hooks one above the other with a 2-ounce sinker, depending on the current. They are rather sporting and will give you a bit of a fight. And you will never find a more delicious fish to put in your frying pan.

HOW TO COOK KINGFISH

CONSCIENCE POINT KINGFISH

6 medium-sized kingfish (¾ to 1 pound)
¼ cup flour
¼ cup seasoned bread crumbs
¼ cup butter
¼ cup olive oil
3 tablespoons capers
½ cup wine

Roll or shake the fish in the flour and crumb mixture. Fry in the oil and butter until tan. Just before serving, sprinkle with the capers and wine. Serves 6.

CUTCHOGUE KINGFISH

2 kingfish (about 1 pound each)
½ cup white wine (I rather like Chablis for fish cookery.)
2 tablespoons butter
1 teaspoon salad herbs

Place cleaned fish in a buttered baking dish. Add the white wine, butter, and herbs and bake at 400° for 25 minutes. Serves 2.

HOG NECK KINGFISH

1 2-pound kingfish
2 whole tomatoes stuffed with bread crumbs
2 carrots, diced fine
1 cup fresh peas
2 tablespoons lemon juice
¼ teaspoon salt
⅛ teaspoon pepper
4 tablespoons butter

Place the fish in a buttered or foil-lined pan. Attractively arrange the vegetables around the fish. Sprinkle with the salt, pepper, and lemon juice and dot with butter. Bake at 400° for 30 minutes and serve in the same pan. Serves 2 to 3.

JEAN'S KINGFISH

4 fillets of kingfish or small whole ones
½ cup butter
1 cup toasted coconut
½ cup white wine

Melt part of the butter in the bottom of a broiling pan. Add the fish and the rest of the butter. Broil for 8 minutes. Add the coconut and the wine, baste, and broil for 8 minutes more. Serves 4.

MIDDLE GROUNDS KINGFISH

8 small kingfish
4 tablespoons olive oil
1 clove garlic, crushed
¼ teaspoon seafood seasoning
2 tablespoons chopped parsley

Heat the olive oil and the crushed garlic. Sprinkle the seafood seasoning and parsley on the fish and sauté until brown, about 8 to 12 minutes on each side. Serves 8.

NASSAU POINT KINGFISH

2 ½- to 1-pound kingfish
16 strips salt pork (1-inch squares cut in half and thinly sliced)
¼ teaspoon salt
⅛ teaspoon pepper
4 tablespoons lemon juice

Clean and wash the kingfish. Rub salt in the cavity. Cut slits, about eight of them, slantwise on the top of each fish. Insert a strip of salt pork in each slit. Sprinkle with salt, pepper, and lemon juice. Place in a foil-lined broiler. Broil for exactly 20 minutes. The salt pork and the skin will be a delicious, crisp brown, and the inside will be white, tender, and juicy. The combination of salt pork and fish is unusually good. They seem to complement each other. Serves 2.

I truly think that this is one of my best recipes!

STELLA'S BROILED KINGFISH WITH DILL

4 ½- to 1-pound kingfish
4 tablespoons butter
4 tablespoons dill
4 tablespoons lemon juice
¼ teaspoon salt

Arrange split kingfish in a broiler pan that has been lined with foil. Dot with butter and sprinkle with salt, dill, and lemon juice. Broil for about 16 minutes, or until golden. Serves 4.

THREE-MILE KINGFISH

4 kingfish
½ cup white wine
2 tablespoons chopped parsley
2 cloves garlic, crushed
¼ cup olive oil
½ teaspoon orégano

Place the fish in a buttered baking dish. Blend wine, parsley, garlic, olive oil, and orégano and pour over the fish. Bake at 400° for 25 minutes. Baste once in a while. Serves 4.

Eels

The first eel I ever caught was quite by accident, and I never really cared if I ever caught another one. I was fishing for snappers with a bamboo pole when I hooked a monster eel. The pole almost bent in half; in fact, I don't know why it didn't break. When I swung back with all my might, a big black wiggling "thing" was at my feet. My little dog almost went crazy, and so did I! I guess you could hear me screaming in Connecticut. Anyhow, my husband heard me and came to my rescue.

He released "it" from the hook and took it home and skinned it. The next morning I cut the eel in pieces, rolled it in fine crumbs, and fried it. My family said it was delicious. I wouldn't know, because I left the room when the pieces began to wiggle in the pan.

However, under coercion from my editor I have since learned to prepare them to avoid that kind of thing, and I am more than happy to pass my information on to you because I have really learned to love *eels*.

HOW TO CATCH EELS

Eels are found in creeks, bays, rivers, and sounds. A favorite sport is spearing or jacking at night. You paddle quietly in a boat and spot the eels with a gasoline lantern, and fast like a bunny you jab them with a spear. You can buy eel spears. You can also fish for them using killies or bloodworms for bait on a light boat rod with a No. 9 hook and enough of a sinker to allow the line to rest on the bottom.

Or you can buy such a contraption as an eel trap. They are really kind of fun to catch. One night last summer four of us piled in a small boat and went eeling. It was quite hilarious, as the men delighted in tossing the speared eels into the women's laps. The other gal jumped overboard when an eel hit her. I bore up under the strain, as I knew I had to catch an eel to tell you how to do it!

HOW TO SKIN EELS

Since eels are such slippery, slimy creatures, a good trick to know is to rub sand on your hands to help you hold them. Slit the neck of the eel and tie a string around it. Fasten the string to a nail or a hook and with the aid of pliers pull off the skin. Slit the stomach and remove the entrails. Wash.

Cut the eel in two-inch pieces and slit along the backbone of each piece. This little trick cuts the muscle so that the pieces will not jump in the frying pan. Also, it is a good idea to parboil the eel chunks for two or three minutes before cooking. I had to do this to try the recipes and, believe it or not, it really works and I will catch, cook, and eat an eel any day.

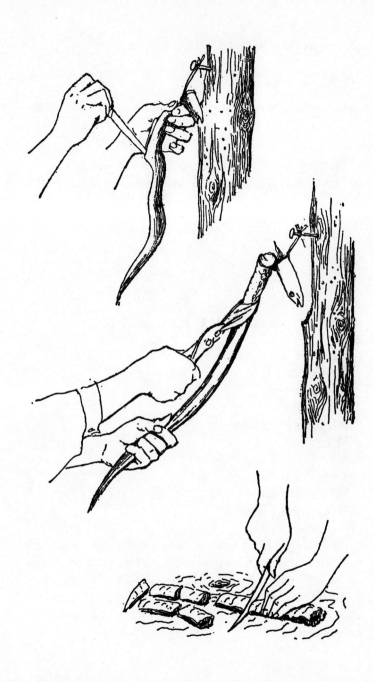

HOW TO COOK EELS

The number of servings depends on the size of the eel, of course, but in general you should allow a half pound per person.

THELMA MARCY'S EEL ASPIC

1 eel, cut in 1½-inch pieces
1 tablespoon pickling spices tied in a bag
½ cup vinegar
1 cup water
1 tablespoon gelatin
¼ cup water
2 hard-cooked eggs, quartered
2 small tomatoes, quartered
¼ teaspoon salt
⅛ teaspoon pepper

Cover the eel slices with the vinegar and 1 cup water. Add the spice bag. Simmer for 20 minutes. Add the gelatin softened in ¼ cup water. In a mold, arrange the eel, eggs, and tomatoes attractively. Remove the spice bag and pour the cooled cooked liquid over the arrangement. Chill until firm. Serve on lettuce.

EELS WITH TOMATO SAUCE

1 eel, cut in pieces
1 onion, sliced thin
1 teaspoon sugar
¼ teaspoon salt
⅛ teaspoon pepper
½ teaspoon basil
½ teaspoon orégano
1 6-ounce can tomato sauce

Layer the eel and the onion slices in a baking dish. Sprinkle with sugar, salt, pepper, basil, orégano, and tomato sauce. Bake at 400° for 30 minutes.

MARIANI'S EELS

1 prepared eel, cut in pieces
1 pound can tomatoes
2 cloves garlic, crushed
1 teaspoon sugar
¼ teaspoon salt
⅛ teaspoon pepper
2 tablespoons chopped parsley

Simmer the tomatoes, garlic, sugar, salt, pepper, and parsley for 20 minutes. Add the eel and simmer for another 20 minutes.

MATTITUCK EEL STEW

1 eel, cleaned, cut in pieces, and browned in fat
4 potatoes, sliced
2 onions, sliced
¼ teaspoon salt
⅛ teaspoon pepper

In a casserole, layer potato and onion slices. Place browned eel on the top. Season. Add enough water to cover. Cover tightly and bake at 350° until potatoes are tender. Serves 2 to 4, depending, of course, on the size of the eel.

NORTH SEA EEL

1 prepared eel, cut in pieces
½ cup olive oil
2 cloves garlic, crushed
1 tablespoon chopped parsley
1 tablespoon lemon juice
tiny pinch red pepper
¼ teaspoon salt
⅛ teaspoon pepper

Combine the oil, garlic, parsley, lemon juice, and seasonings. Marinate the eel in this mixture for at least 15 minutes —the longer, the better. Place in a broiler pan and broil for about 5 minutes on each side.

PIERRE'S FRIED EELS

1 eel, cut in 2-inch pieces
1 egg, slightly beaten
½ cup flour
¼ teaspoon salt
⅛ teaspoon pepper
fat or oil for frying

Parboil eel for 3 minutes. Dip in egg, then roll in flour seasoned with salt and pepper. Fry for 5 minutes on each side.

SUE'S BAKED EEL

1 eel, cut in 1½-inch pieces
2 onions, sliced

Put the onions in the bottom of a baking pan. Place the pieces of eel on top. Bake at 375° for 25 to 30 minutes. Don't peek, as the eel might be squirming. This is another one of those little tricks I was telling you about. When the eel is done, remove from the oven and discard the onions. Since eels are oily, the onion absorbs some of the oil and eels are very crisp and nice this way. It works!

ANGUILLES AU VERT
A LA FLAMANDE
(EELS FLEMISH STYLE)

I like other people's food, especially Mrs. Pagani's of the
Brussels Restaurant. Miss Clara Claasen and I enjoyed the
eels vert so much at her restaurant that she graciously sent
me her recipe.

2 pounds eel
½ cup butter
1 onion
2 shallots
2 stalks celery
5 ounces sorrel
5 ounces watercress
⅓ ounce parsley
⅓ ounce chervil
⅙ ounce sage
⅙ ounce mint
⅙ ounce savory
white dry wine
¼ teaspoon salt
⅛ teaspoon pepper
⅛ teaspoon nutmeg
juice of 1 lemon
2 egg yolks
1 teaspoon fecula (potato flour)

Cut up eel in pieces about 2½ inches long. Fry them
lightly in simmering butter with finely cut onions, shallots,
and celery. Season, and add finely cut sorrel, watercress, parsley, chervil, and a little cheesecloth bag containing sage,

mint, and savory. (The amounts in this recipe are for each 2 pounds of eel.)

Cook very rapidly for 12 to 15 minutes and then moisten with enough dry white wine to cover all the pieces. Season with salt, pepper, and nutmeg.

In a porcelain container, press the juice of a lemon. Add egg yolks, fecula, and dilute with the fish broth (strained from the cooking of the eels). Then add the eels, mix, and let cool. This dish can be eaten warm as well as cold. As an appetizer, it serves 8 to 12; as a main course, it serves 4 to 6.

Tuna

Recently a bunch of us went to Montauk to gather blue-berries. Blueberry bushes out that way grow taller than people and are so full of luscious berries that they are purple in July. So it is our custom, when we find they are ripe, to go gathering. Montauk berries make the finest pancakes, roly poly, cakes, and muffins ever.

As we were leaving for Montauk a neighbor asked us to buy a small tuna for her for her freezer. So after we had picked enough berries we went to the dock to watch the fishing boats come in and to buy fish for our own picnic supper and to accomplish the errand for our neighbor.

Since it was rather late on a Friday afternoon, all they had for sale was one 20-pound tuna and 2 small flukes. We grabbed all and stashed them in the car.

We parked the car on a dune overlooking a blue, blue sea and dragged a grill with fire makings, a tossed salad, potato chips, and the filleted flukes to the beach.

I spread mayonnaise on the fillets and broiled them over white coals. They were delicious but not quite satisfactory enough for our enormous appetites, and the same thought occurred to all of us: What were we doing going hungry when we had 20 pounds of tuna in the car?

It wasn't long before we had hacked away a mess of tuna steaks and had them on the fire. I drenched them with the

French dressing I had for the tossed salad, covered them with mayonnaise, and charcoaled them for 12 minutes on each side. Well, I'll tell you nothing—but nothing—ever tasted so good.

Of course we were a little sheepish when we brought back half of a tuna, but we had discovered a marvelous recipe!

Unless tuna is extremely fresh, it is better to soak it in milk before preparing the following recipes, otherwise it acquires an oily, strong taste.

HOW TO COOK TUNA

AMAGANSETT TUNA STEAKS

    2 1-inch center-cut tuna steaks
    1 cup sliced onions
    3 tablespoons olive oil
    1 tablespoon vinegar
    ¼ teaspoon salt
    ⅛ teaspoon pepper
    ½ teaspoon orégano

Sauté the onions in the hot oil in a frying pan until they are yellow. Add the steaks, vinegar, and the seasonings. Cover and steam for 20 minutes.

ANCHOVY TUNA

4 tuna steaks
1 cup medium white sauce
1 tablespoon anchovy paste
½ cup black pitted olives
½ cup mayonnaise

Mix the white sauce, anchovy paste, black olives, and mayonnaise. Spread on the steaks and bake at 400° for 25 minutes. This is awfully good spread on almost any whole fish. Serves 4.

NAPEAQUE TUNA

1 pound tuna steaks, cut in chunks
¼ cup cooking oil
1 clove garlic, crushed
1 cup chopped green peppers
1 cup chopped onion
½ cup chopped celery
1 tablespoon cornstarch
1 cup water
1 tablespoon soy sauce
¼ teaspoon salt
2 tomatoes, quartered

Brown the tuna, garlic, peppers, onion, and celery in the oil. Add more oil if needed. Smooth cornstarch with the water and add with remaining ingredients. Cover. Cook for 45 minutes. Serve on rice. Serves 4.

BLOCK ISLAND BROILED TUNA

2 1-inch tuna steaks
1 teaspoon seasoned salt or fish seasoning
2 tablespoons butter
2 tablespoons lemon juice

Season steaks. Cover with butter and sprinkle with lemon juice. Broil under a broiler or outside over a fire for 10 to 12 minutes on each side. Serves 2 to 4, depending on the size of the steaks.

DONNE'S CANNED TUNA

This is an old native recipe from Long Island. I did not prepare this myself, but I have a friend who does this every year and I think it is marvelous and well worth the effort in case someone brings home a tuna. It is very good for an appetizer, lunch, casseroles, and so on.

Clean, wash, and drain a freshly caught tuna. Steam until cooked. Chill for 6 to 12 hours. Cut in chunk-sized pieces. Pack in hot pint jars. Add 1 teaspoon salt and 2 tablespoons of salad dressing to each jar. Process for 90 minutes at 10 pounds pressure. Then screw lid tight.

Donne's Tuna is wonderful spread on crackers for an appetizer with cocktails. It also makes a delicious salad or sandwich.

MONTAUK TUNA STEAKS

1-inch tuna steaks
2 tablespoons French or Italian salad dressing per steak
2 tablespoons mayonnaise per steak

Drench one side of the steak with French or Italian salad dressing and spread with mayonnaise. Place in a hand grill and cook over charcoal for 10 to 12 minutes with the spread side down. Turn, spread the other side the same way, and grill. Steaks near the middle of the tuna will serve 2, and steaks near the end will serve 1.

Swordfish

Because swordfish is so popular and so easy to obtain in most stores and is so good when it is fresh, I would like to include a few of my favorite recipes. Perhaps someday I may catch one, who knows? I think if one took a poll the dear old swordfish would win—first because it has no bones, and second because it is really unsurpassed in flavor and texture.

It is terribly good just plain broiled. Spread the steak with butter and broil under the broiler for about 8 minutes on each side. Sprinkle with paprika and serve with lemon wedges. Or spread with mayonnaise and broil under the broiler outside.

I have a friend from Connecticut who claims that the only way to cook swordfish is to spread with butter or mayonnaise and broil in a hand grill, turning often. It does taste wonderful with that charcoal flavor.

Or melt the butter in a pan as described for Eleanor's Flounder Fillets and broil. It does no harm to sauté swordfish on top of the stove in butter. However, I think that its own flavor is so fine that it does not need a rich sauce or too many embellishments. Remember, it is fun to fool around with different herbs, spices, and seasonings. There are some fish sauces on the market that are absolutely wonderful. Try spreading some of these on that swordfish and see what happens. The good fish cook is one who will experiment and use her imagination.

HOW TO COOK SWORDFISH

AMAGANSETT SWORDFISH

2 to 3 pounds swordfish
¼ pound butter
2 tablespoons chopped dill

Melt the butter in a frying pan. Add the dill and the fish. Cover pan and cook for 10 minutes. Remove the cover and brown for 5 minutes on each side. Serves 4 to 6.

PORTUGUESE SWORDFISH

1 pound swordfish, cut in pieces
1 green pepper, cut in strips
1 onion, sliced
½ pound mushrooms, sliced
½ cup olive oil
¼ teaspoon salt
⅛ teaspoon pepper
¼ teaspoon orégano
¼ teaspoon paprika
2 cans anchovies

Sauté the green pepper, onion, and mushrooms in the olive oil. Add the swordfish and brown. Add the seasonings and anchovies. Cover the pan and steam for 10 minutes. Serves 3 to 4.

BRIDGEHAMPTON SWORDFISH

3 pounds swordfish steaks
6 tablespoons salad dressing
6 tablespoons mayonnaise

Spread the steaks with the dressing and mayonnaise. Place in a hand grill and broil over the coals for 8 to 10 minutes on each side. Sprinkle with seasoned salt and serve with lemon slices. Serves 6.

Weakfish

For years I heard my father tell stories about the great weakfish runs in Peconic Bay on Long Island. So when we moved in front of the weakfish grounds it became my burning ambition to catch one. The days of the great runs seem to be over, but in the early spring and fall one can catch these fish.

I truly think they are beautiful. Fresh-caught, they have a gold and blue coloring that is lovely, and the orange fin is a charming contrast. They are spotted like trout and are sometimes called sea trout. The meat is fine-grained and a little on the dark side. They run in size from 1 pound up, the average in my neck of the woods being about 2 to 4 pounds. I know of no finer eating than a 2-pound weakfish, split, boned, doused with plenty of butter, and broiled. The weaks, kings, and blues are my favorites, and each year when I try to decide which kind I like the best I simply can't do it.

HOW TO CATCH WEAKFISH

Most of the time I fish for weakfish just up from the bottom, but they are also caught by trolling and drifting. There is a rig called a Peconic "Hi Lo" that is used in the bay. The top hook is several feet above the sinker and has a long leader; the bottom hook is just above the sinker. Squid, bloodworms, and clams are the bait; their favorite is the bloodworm.

The weakfish hang out above the bottom of the bay, so it is suggested that you let the sinker rest on the bottom and gently lift it up in a rhythmic motion and reel in occasionally. The reason for this is that they may have been eying your bait, and the movement may give them the urge to grab, plus the fact that they swim up a little. Weaks are a game fish and they warily eye the bait and than strike when it moves. This is also the principle of drifting. Apparently the movement attracts them. If you get a strike and don't hook or boat him the first time, let your line sink back gently in the same spot. They often strike twice at the same bait. At least that is what it feels like. Who knows? It may be another fish, but I can't see the bottom of the bay.

Many men cast for these fish from the shores of the bay just before sundown. They use a light spinning rod and a feather. Since I am not going to have a boat next year, I am going to concentrate on this method.

But I must warn you, never, never go weakfishing without a landing net. They are called weakfish for a reason. They have a very weak mouth, they are fighters, and they can tear themselves away from the hook. So always have a net handy to scoop them up and bring them in.

HOW TO COOK WEAKFISH

ITALIAN BAKED WEAKFISH

1 2- to 3-pound weakfish, cleaned and left whole
1½ cups Italian Stuffing
1 tomato, quartered
¼ cup Italian salad dressing

Place the fish in a baking pan. Fill the cavity with the stuffing. Place the tomato wedges on the top. Pour the salad dressing on top and bake at 350° for 45 to 60 minutes. Serves 4 to 5.

ITALIAN STUFFING

1½ cups seasoned bread crumbs
2 tablespoons parsley
2 tablespoons grated Romano cheese
1 clove garlic, crushed
3 tablespoons olive oil

Mix everything together well.

BARBECUED WEAKFISH

  2 medium weakfish, cleaned and left whole
  ¼ onion minced
  2 tablespoons salad oil
  2 tablespoons catsup
  2 tablespoons vinegar
  2 tablespoons brown sugar
  1 teaspoon Worcestershire sauce
  1 teaspoon mustard
  ¼ teaspoon salt
  ⅛ teaspoon pepper

Combine everything except the fish and mix well. Marinate the fish in the mixture for at least an hour, turning once. Place in a hand grill and broil over the coals about 8 minutes on each side, basting with the sauce. Serves 2 to 4.

GIN LANE WEAKFISH

  1 1½- to 2-pound weakfish, cleaned and split
  ½ cup butter
  1 cup seedless grapes
  ¼ cup white wine

Place the fish in a broiling pan. Spread ¼ cup butter on top and broil for 8 to 10 minutes. Turn and spread with the remaining butter. Add grapes and wine and broil for 8 minutes more. Do not open this fish or spread it out. Leave it whole. It is very elegant. Serves 2.

This recipe is good with kings, striped bass, or any fillets.

PECONIC BAY WEAKFISH

1 1- to 2-pound weakfish
1 cup fine, seasoned bread crumbs
½ teaspoon orégano
2 cloves garlic, crushed
2 tablespoons olive oil

Clean, split, and bone the weakfish. Place spread open in a broiling pan. Mix crumbs, orégano, garlic, and olive oil. Spread on the fish. Broil for 15 to 18 minutes. Serves 2 to 3.

RIVERHEAD WEAKFISH

1 3- to 4-pound weakfish
¼ pound salt pork, cut in strips
1 cup Weakfish Stuffing
2 tablespoons lemon juice

Clean weakfish. Cut gashes on top about an inch apart and tuck pieces of salt pork in each gash. Fill the cavity with the stuffing. Sprinkle with lemon juice and bake at 400° for about 45 minutes. Serves 4.

When I bake a fish I leave the head on. Tuck some parsley around the head and put a lemon slice or an olive over the eye. When you have something as special as this, particularly if you caught it, serve it with style and dash!

ROSE GROVE BAKED WEAKFISH

    1 2- to 4-pound weakfish
    1 cup Weakfish Stuffing
    ½ teaspoon salt
    2 tablespoons lemon juice
    2 strips bacon

Clean the fish. Rub the cavity and body with salt. Put the stuffing in the cavity. Place in a baking pan lined with foil. Sprinkle with lemon juice and put the strips of bacon on top. Bake at 400° for about 25 minutes. Serves 3 to 4.

WOOLEY POND BROILED WEAKFISH

    1 1½- to 2-pound weakfish
    4 tablespoons butter
    2 tablespoons lemon juice
    1 teaspoon chopped parsley
    ¼ teaspoon fish seasoning

Clean and split the weakfish. Place in a broiler pan. Dot with butter, sprinkle with the lemon juice, parsley, and fish seasoning. Broil for about 15 minutes. Serves 2 if you are nice and hungry, and you will be if you caught the fish!

WEAKFISH STUFFING

1 tablespoon chopped onion
1 tablespoon bacon fat
1 cup seasoned stuffing
1 tablespoon parsley
2 tablespoons water

Sauté the onion in the bacon fat until onion is yellow. Add the stuffing, parsley, and water and mix well. This is a good stuffing for all kinds of fish.

Striped Bass

THE BIG ONE THAT GOT AWAY

Off Cow Neck, where the two Peconic bays greet one another, lie the local, handsome stripers—that is, striped bass or
rock, as they are called farther south. They run from only
2 to about 5 pounds in size but are tremendously gamey to
catch and terrific to eat. Men stand on shore and cast all
night for these handsome fish, or they troll from sunset well
into dark near the shore. They are a challenge, an addiction,
a disease. Catching them gets into the blood.

Tremendous ones run off Montauk in the late fall at
about the same time as the large blues, until November,
when the cod start to run.

The beautiful, bright October day when I caught my first
large blue proved to be very exciting. My son was in the fishing chair when suddenly his rod took a big dip. It was no
ordinary fish, because Joel has powerful shoulders and arms,
and it took all his strength to bring the tip of the rod up.
The captain and the mate yelled "Cow!" With that, the
action began. Joel played the fish and had the thrill of his
life, and so did we onlookers. I don't know how long the

skillful teamwork among Joel, the captain, mate, and fish lasted, but victory started to become Joel's when to our absolute horror another charter boat ran right over the line. We waved, exhorted, pleaded, swore, but the fishermen in the stern heeded us not and let the boat continue. Well, you know what happened. The next weekend my son went back to get the fish or the captain, I know not which. Anyhow, everyone on the boat thought a real prize size had got away.

I'd like to add a postscript. In October 1960, I caught my first striped bass at about the same spot that Joel lost his, and it weighed 39 pounds and 12 ounces. If you don't believe me, I have a picture to prove it and a certificate of award from the Ruppert's contest. I shall have to rest on my laurels because I can never duplicate that thrill, amazement, surprise, and delight.

HOW TO CATCH STRIPED BASS

When I wrote the striped bass chapter the summer of 1960 I said I couldn't tell a soul how to catch a striped bass because it was the dream of my life.

On the first of October my son said he wanted to close the cottage because he had received Uncle Sam's greetings and he had other things on his mind. My face and spirits fell because I hadn't been deep-sea fishing and the big blues and the bass were running.

So I drooped and hinted that I needed a bass to test some recipes and that he was just the boy to catch one. Now that young man loves fishing and particularly fishing for striped bass, so before long I was on the phone arranging for a split charter at Montauk for the next morning.

We went out on a boat with two men. When we reached the fishing grounds one said, "Lady, are you going to fish?" I shyly nodded and said, "But you men start." There were three fishing chairs on the boat, you see, and *four* of us, and I truly didn't want to get in the way, but still I wanted to fish.

We trolled for about an hour, using white, yellow, and blue feathers with pork rind in the hook. We went back and forth past the lighthouse, and all that we caught was one blue. We watched the other boats, and they weren't doing much either. It looked as if it was going to be a slow day.

The captain had us pull in the lines so that he could speed up the boat and change course. We went around the lighthouse and headed west, staying close to shore. We slowed to trolling speed again and dropped the hooks. I smelled watermelon, so my nose and pulse twitched. I just *felt* fish.

Before long Joel pulled in a nice striper, about 10 to 15 pounds, and so did one of the other men, and several nice blues were boated. The action was getting good.

Suddenly a man's rod tip bent way down and someone yelled "Cow!" And sure enough, after a beautiful relationship among boat, captain, mate, fish, and fisherman, a gorgeous 20-pound "cow" was gaffed. I had never seen one that large, so I was terribly impressed and so was the man who caught it. He said he had been fishing for one like that all of his life.

It wasn't five minutes later that my rod bent and I knew I had something big on the line. Somebody said, "Oh, she just caught the bottom." But the mate felt the line and shook his head. Then everything broke loose. Somebody wanted to hold my shoulders; somebody else wanted to hold my feet. I know they all wanted to take the rod. But I gritted my teeth, firmed my body, tightened my grip, and said, "I want to get this one in all by myself." So I reeled and reeled and reeled with all my might. I wouldn't even look up for fear I'd slacken. I have no idea how long it took. Once in a while the fish sounded, and he was so heavy I thought I had the whole bottom of the ocean. Then when he came up and swam toward the boat I was afraid I'd lost him and I reeled like a demon. Finally somebody yelled, "I see him, and what a monster." Out of the corner of my eye I saw the mate reach for the gaff. Just a few more long, hard turns and there it was! I never knew they came that big. If I had— well, we won't go into that.

We rode back to the dock, tired but happy. When we weighed in, my son winked at me and said, "Mother, men won't like you!"

HOW TO COOK STRIPED BASS

COW NECK STRIPED BASS

4 inch-thick bass steaks or a medium-sized whole bass
1 teaspoon fish seasoning
4 tablespoons Italian dressing or French salad dressing

Sprinkle fish with the seasoning. Place in a broiler, inside or out. Put half of the salad dressing on top of the fish. Broil for 8 minutes. Turn. Add the other half of the dressing and broil for 8 minutes more. If the fish is larger and is not done, broil longer but be sure that you don't overcook it. If you broil over a charcoal fire, be sure to use a hand grill so that you do not break the fish when you turn them. Serves 4.

BLOCK ISLAND SOUND STRIPED BASS

    4 bass steaks
    4 tablespoons butter
    1 medium onion, chopped fine
    ½ green pepper, chopped fine
    2 tomatoes, chopped
    1 cup white wine
    1 tablespoon A.1. sauce
    ¼ teaspoon salt
    ⅛ teaspoon pepper

Place the steaks in a buttered baking pan. Spread half the butter on the top and brown under the broiler. In the meantime cook the onion and green pepper in the rest of the butter until the onion is brown or rather transparent. Add the tomatoes, wine, A.1. sauce, salt, and pepper. Pour this mixture over the bass and bake at 375° for 30 minutes. Serves 4.

LIGHTHOUSE STRIPED BASS

    1 7- to 10-pound striped bass
    1½ cups fish stuffing
    ½ pound butter, melted

Stuff the bass with Bluefish Stuffing or Weakfish Stuffing and place on a rack in a baking pan with a little water in the bottom. Bake at 275° for 2½ hours, basting frequently with the ½ pound of butter. When done, garnish with parsley and lemon quarters and serve with parsley potatoes on the side. Serves 6 to 8.

MAIDSTONE STRIPED BASS

6 ½-pound striped bass steaks
¼ pound butter
1 shallot, minced, or 1 tablespoon chives, chopped
1 tablespoon flour
1 split champagne (⅔ pint)
1 tablespoon chopped parsley
6 slivers of lemon peel
¼ teaspoon salt
⅛ teaspoon pepper

Melt the butter in a large skillet. Lightly brown the steaks, turning once. Remove the steaks. In the drippings in the pan stir the shallots and flour until brown. Add the champagne, salt and pepper, and stir until the mixture thickens. Place the bass in the sauce. Cover and cook until flaky, about 5 to 10 minutes. Just before serving, add the parsley and lemon peel. This is so elegant and so good you will impress your friends no end! Serves 6.

MONTAUK STRIPED BASS

2 pounds striped bass, cut into steaks
1 cup medium white sauce
½ cup mayonnaise
¼ cup lemon juice
1 tablespoon chives
¼ cup white wine, if desired
1 tablespoon butter

Place the steaks in a buttered casserole. Mix the white sauce, mayonnaise, lemon juice, chives, and white wine and pour over the fish. Dot with butter and bake at 400° for 25 to 30 minutes. I think this is my favorite striped bass recipe. The flavor is marvelous, though rich! Serves 4.

STRIPED BASS WITH MUSTARD SAUCE

2 pounds striped bass steaks
3 tablespoons butter
3 tablespoons finely chopped onion
2 tablespoons prepared mustard
¼ teaspoon salt
⅛ teaspoon pepper
½ cup heavy cream
½ cup white wine

Place the fish steaks in a buttered baking dish. Melt the butter in a saucepan, and sauté onion until it is yellow. Blend the mustard, salt, pepper, and cream in the butter and onion mixture. Pour this over the fish. Add the wine. Bake at 375° for 30 minutes. Serves 4.

PETER L'S STRIPED BASS

1 whole striped bass, about 2 pounds
1 Bermuda onion, cut in rings
4 carrots cut in strips
4 celery stalks
2 bay leaves
¼ teaspoon salt
⅛ teaspoon pepper
½ cup butter
½ cup sauterne

Place the bass in a fish casserole. Surround it with the onion rings, carrots, and celery strips. Sprinkle with the bay leaves, salt, and pepper. Cover with butter and bake at 400° for 45 minutes. About 5 minutes before done, pour on the sauterne. Serves 4.

THE MIDDLE GROUNDS BAKED FISH GOOD FOR STRIPER, BLUE, TUNA, OR ANY OTHER FISH STEAK

2 to 4 fish steaks
4 tablespoons melted butter
1 cup canned tomatoes, drained
½ teaspoon sugar
½ onion, sliced
¼ teaspoon salt
⅛ teaspoon pepper
½ cup heavy cream

Place fish steaks in a buttered or foil-lined baking dish. Pour the melted butter over them. Spread with canned tomatoes. Sprinkle with sugar. Put the onion slices on the top. Sprinkle with salt and pepper. Cover with the cream. Bake at 375° for 25 to 30 minutes. Serves 2 to 4, depending on the size of the steaks.

I think people who love fish could eat ½ pound. For anyone who is lukewarm about them, allow less—but with good *fresh* fish and a good recipe, see what happens!

BAKED STRIPED BASS

1 striped bass (about 10 pounds)
1½ cups stuffing
¼ teaspoon salt
⅛ teaspoon pepper
4 strips bacon
4 slices onion
4 slices tomato
parsley and lemon slices

Clean the fish without removing the head. Fill the cavity with the stuffing (see weakfish). Sprinkle salt and pepper on the fish. Put in a large baking pan and alternate the bacon, onion, and tomato slices on top. Bake at 350° for about 60 minutes. Test with a fork to see if the meat flakes easily and peek to see if it is as white as new snow. If this is the case, the fish is done. This test is good for any kind of fish.

Serve with aplomb on a large platter with a lemon slice over the eye and surround the fish with parsley and lemon slices. A bass this size serves 4 to 6. Remember, the head and tail are waste.

Flotsam and Jetsam

One bright September day we were on the prowl for the big blues. We trolled Plum Gut, between Long Island Sound and Gardiners Bay, the Race, and various other spots unsuccessfully. A certain member of my family dislikes bottom fishing, so I sneaked my little boat rod, squid, and bottom tackle and hid it in the boat.

After we explored the Old Fort in Gardiners Bay, I produced my equipment. We threw out the anchor and proceeded to go for the nice big sea bass that hang out in the area. I no sooner got the hook on the bottom than my rod bent as I have never seen it bend before. I reeled and fought with all my might, and to our surprise I hauled in a three-foot sand shark. We knocked it on the head and tossed it in the bottom of the boat to bring back to show our friends. I cast out again, and I think before the hook reached the bottom the same thing happened, only this time the rod bent over farther and the monster seemed heavier. I was weak from laughter and fighting and I couldn't reel in any more, so I handed my rod over, and to our intense surprise we hauled in a shark that was half the size of our boat, about 6 feet. We conked that one and let it join the other on the boat bottom, when to our amazement *she* began to have babies. It was quite an experience.

I have a theory that everything that comes from the sea is edible if only you know how to prepare it. So when we tied up at Sag Harbor to get gas and everyone came to gape at the fishes, I inquired whether shark was good to eat and how one would go about cleaning and cooking it. All I learned was that someone heard it made good stew! However, when later we caught some more, I experimented, and herewith are the recipes.

I have read an article that explained that the old sea robin is good to eat too. After all, who was the first to try an eel?

SHARK

OLD FORT SHARK STEAKS

4 shark steaks, 1 inch thick
⅛ pound butter
¼ teaspoon salt
⅛ teaspoon pepper
8-ounce can pineapple rings
4 teaspoons coconut chips or shredded coconut

Melt the butter in a frying pan. Brown the steaks on each side in the butter. Add the juice from the can of pineapple. Cover tightly and steam for 5 minutes. Place a pineapple ring on the top of each steak and steam for 5 minutes more. Serve with 1 teaspoon of coconut chips on each steak. Believe it or not, this is pretty good! This is a version of the manner in which the Hawaiian mahi mahi is sometimes prepared and can be made with bonita with great success, or haddock, cod, or striped bass.

SKATE

One day when I went to my favorite fish market to buy some ingredients for bouillabaisse, what did I see but the homely old skate all dressed up and ready to go. I pestered the fish man, and he finally told me how to clean the creature and also how to cook it. The best I could get out of it was that with a pair of good shears the wings are cut out in an arc and skinned. It is hard to explain, but if you had a skate in front of you I think you could see what I mean. I understand the Japanese are very fond of them. So next summer when we are pestered by those things I will astound my friends by bringing skates home and cooking them. One of these days my friends are going to be afraid to visit me!

SHAG WONG SKATE

1 pound skate wings cut in pieces, or about 2 cups
1½ tablespoons vegetable or animal fat for frying
¼ cup chopped onions
½ cup chopped celery
½ cup chopped mushrooms
¼ cup chopped green pepper
¼ teaspoon salt
⅛ teaspoon pepper
¼ cup water

THICKENING SAUCE

1½ tablespoons cornstarch
½ teaspoon sugar
1 tablespoon La Choy sauce

Heat the fat in a skillet. Add the fish and onions and cook until the onions are yellow. Add the celery, mushrooms, green pepper, salt, pepper, and water. Cover and boil for 5 minutes. Add the thickening sauce, stirring until well blended. Serve on rice. Serves 3 to 4.

HOW TO CLEAN SEA ROBIN

The sea robin has terribly spiny fins. In fact, it would be something like grabbing a porcupine! So get out those gloves. With sharp shears cut off all the fins and tails. Then cut off the head and clean out the entrails. Work the skin nearest the head loose and peel the same as you would a blowfish. A solid piece of flesh similar to the flesh of the blowfish will be available, only the sea robin is much larger.

SHINNECOCK SEA ROBIN CASSEROLE

4 cleaned sea robins
1 package dried onion soup
1 cup white wine

Place the sea robins in a casserole. Mix the soup with the wine and pour over the fish. Cover and bake for 25 minutes at 400°. Serves 4.

Casseroles,Chowders,Etc.

I have decided to make a separate chapter of casseroles and chowders because the fish used in both is absolutely interchangeable. Any thick fish steak or fillet can be used for these dishes. For instance, out my way in the summer, flounder, fluke, sea bass, tuna, swordfish, and dolphin are good. In the fall we have the big blues, striped bass, and then cod for the winter. In the stores you can buy cod, haddock, all kinds of fillets, and some of those wonderful fish from the South, such as red snapper. Including the good frozen varieties, you have the world of fish at your fingertips to make delectable, economical, nutritious, delicious casseroles and chowders.

CASSEROLES

ORIENT POINT CASSEROLE

2 cups flaked fish
1 10½-ounce can cream of chicken soup
½ 10½-ounce can milk
1 teaspoon curry powder
½ cup seasoned bread crumbs
2 tablespoons butter or margarine

Combine the fish, soup, milk, and curry powder. Put in a buttered casserole. Cover with the bread crumbs and dot with butter. Bake at 400° for ½ hour. Serves 3 to 4.

AQUEBOGUE CASEROLE

  2 cups fish, diced
  1 1-pound can string beans
  1 10½-ounce can mushroom soup
  ½ 10½-ounce can milk
  ½ cup bread crumbs
  2 tablespoons Parmesan cheese
  ¼ teaspoon salt
  ⅛ teaspoon pepper

Layer fish and string beans in a buttered casserole. Pour the blended soup, salt, pepper, and milk over them. Sprinkle the bread crumbs and cheese on top. Bake at 400° for 25 to 30 minutes. Serves 4. Delicious!

EAST HAMPTON FISH CASSEROLE

  2 cups fish, cut in chunks
  ¼ pound salt pork, diced
  1 onion, chopped
  6 peeled potatoes, diced
  1 pound canned tomatoes
  ¼ teaspoon basil

Fry the salt pork until crisp. Remove from pan. Add onion and cook until yellow. Place half the fish in a buttered casserole; cover with half the salt pork, potatoes, and onion. Repeat. Pour the can of tomatoes over all and sprinkle with the basil. Cover and bake at 375° for 1 hour, or until the potatoes are done. Serves 4 to 6.

PONQUOGUE CASSEROLE

2 pounds fillet of sole
1 10½-ounce can frozen lobster or shrimp soup
½ 10½-ounce can medium cream
6 tablespoons butter
¼ teaspoon salt
⅛ teaspoon pepper
2 tablespoons sherry

Arrange the fillets in a buttered casserole. Smooth the soup with the cream. Pour it over the fillets. Dot with butter. Sprinkle with the salt, pepper, and sherry. Bake at 400° for 30 minutes. Serves 4 to 6.

STELLA'S FISH CASSEROLE

1 pound any nice fish, boned and cut in pieces
1 pound shrimp, cleaned
1 small onion, minced
1 green pepper, minced
½ pound fresh mushrooms, sliced
½ cup butter
1 cup milk
½ cup sherry
1 8-ounce can mushroom soup
1 teaspoon Worcestershire sauce
1½ cups steamed rice

Sauté the fish, onion, green pepper, and mushrooms in the butter until tender. Add the milk, sherry, soup, Worcestershire sauce, and shrimp. Butter a casserole and layer the rice with the fish mixture. Bake at 400° for 25 minutes. Serves 6 to 8.

OYSTER AND FISH CASSEROLE

2 cups fish, cut in chunks (I like to use scissors to cut
  up raw fish.)
1 10½-ounce can frozen oyster soup
1 cup medium cream
1 teaspoon Worcestershire sauce
¼ teaspoon salt
1 teaspoon paprika
⅛ teaspoon pepper
2 tablespoons sherry
½ cup fine bread crumbs
2 tablespoons butter

Mix the oyster soup with the cream, Worcestershire sauce,
salt, paprika, pepper, and sherry. In a buttered casserole,
layer the fish and the soup mixture, ending with the soup.
Cover with bread crumbs and dot with butter. Bake at 400°
for 25 to 30 minutes. Serves 4.

If you can possibly add 1 cup chopped Smithfield or
country ham to this casserole, you will have something fit
for the gods!

WESTHAMPTON FISH CASSEROLE

2 cups fish, cut in pieces
1 10½-ounce can mushroom soup
½ 10½-ounce can milk
2 tablespoons butter
2 tablespoons sherry
¼ teaspoon salt
⅛ teaspoon pepper
⅛ teaspoon nutmeg
2 cups cooked spaghetti
2 tablespoons grated Parmesan cheese
½ cup seasoned, fine bread crumbs

Mix the fish, soup, milk, butter, sherry, salt, pepper, and nutmeg together. Put the spaghetti in a well-buttered casserole. Stir the fish mixture well with the spaghetti. Sprinkle the cheese and bread crumbs on top and bake at 400° for 30 minutes. Serves 4 to 6.

CHOWDERS

ATLANTIC TUNA CHOWDER

2 cups cubed fresh tuna
4 medium onions, chopped
4 strips salt pork
4 diced potatoes
1 cup water
3 cups milk
¼ cup butter
¼ teaspoon salt
⅛ teaspoon pepper
¼ teaspoon paprika

Sauté the onions in the salt pork. Add potatoes and water and boil until the potatoes are tender. Add the tuna and cook until the tuna turns light, about 5 minutes. Add the milk, butter, and seasonings and heat until just under the boiling point. Serves 4 to 6.

NATALIE'S EASY FISH CHOWDER

2 cups fish, cut in chunks (flounder, bass, cod, haddock, etc.)
1 10½-ounce can frozen potato soup
1 10½-ounce can milk
4 tablespoons butter
¼ teaspoon salt
⅛ teaspoon pepper
½ teaspoon paprika or seafood seasoning

Dump the can of potato soup in a saucepan. Add everything else and simmer for 10 to 15 minutes, depending on the fish. Serve with chowder crackers or French bread. Serves 4.

QUOGUE CHOWDER

    2 cups fish, cut in pieces
    1 medium onion, chopped
    ½ medium green pepper, chopped
    1 clove garlic, crushed
    ¼ cup butter
    1 chicken bouillon cube
    1 cup boiling water
    1 1-pound can tomatoes
    1 8-ounce can corn
    ¼ teaspoon salt
    ¼ teaspoon thyme
    ¼ teaspoon basil

Cook the onion, green pepper, and garlic in the butter
until soft. Add the bouillon cube, water, fish, tomatoes, corn,
and seasonings. Simmer gently for 15 minutes. Serves 6 or
so.

ETC.

SOUTHAMPTON SHORES SOUP

    1 10½-ounce can mushroom soup
    1 10½-ounce can asparagus soup
    1 10½-ounce can milk
    1 10½-ounce can water
    2 tablespoons sherry
    2 tablespoons butter
    2 cups flaked fish, cooked or raw

Blend all the ingredients and simmer for 10 minutes.
Serve with pilot crackers. Serves 4 to 6.

SHINNECOCK SOUP

1 cup fish, cut in chunks
1 10½-ounce can mushroom soup
1 10½-ounce can cream of tomato soup
2 10½-ounce cans water
¼ teaspoon paprika
¼ teaspoon curry
¼ teaspoon fish seasoning
¼ teaspoon salt
⅛ teaspoon pepper
2 tablespoons butter

Empty all the cans of soup into a saucepan. Add the water, fish, and all the seasonings. Simmer for 10 minutes. Add the butter and let it melt. Serve with a round of lemon in the bowl. Serves 6 to 8.

FISH SALAD

2 cups cold, cubed cooked fish
½ 10½-ounce can tomato soup
½ cup mayonnaise
¼ cup chopped pickles
1 tablespoon lemon juice
½ teaspoon prepared mustard
½ teaspoon chopped onion
hard-cooked eggs for garnish

Blend the tomato soup with the mayonnaise until smooth. Add the pickles, lemon juice, mustard, and onion. Mix well with the fish cubes and serve on a bed of lettuce. Garnish with slices of hard-cooked eggs. Serves 2 to 4.

JAN'S HALIBUT LOAF

1 pound halibut put through the grinder
1 cup medium cream
1½ cups soft bread crumbs
½ teaspoon salt
1 teaspoon celery seed
1 teaspoon butter
5 egg whites, beaten stiff

In a double boiler, gently cook the cream and bread crumbs for a few minutes. Add the seasonings, butter, and fish. Cool. Add the egg whites. Put in a buttered casserole or loaf pan. Bake in a pan of water in a slow oven, 325°, for 1 hour. Serve with the following sauce:

1 tablespoon flour
1 tablespoon butter
1 pint medium cream, or half cream and half milk
½ cup almonds browned in butter

Melt the butter; add the flour and smooth. Add the cream and cook until creamy. Pour over the loaf and sprinkle the almonds on top when serving. Serves 4 to 6.

FISH SOUFFLÉ

1 pound fillet of sole
½ cup white wine
2 tablespoons butter
1 tablespoon flour
1 cup milk
¼ teaspoon salt
⅛ teaspoon pepper
¼ teaspoon paprika
2 beaten egg yolks
2 beaten egg whites
2 cups mashed potatoes
1 tablespoon seasoned bread crumbs
1 tablespoon grated cheese

Simmer the sole in the white wine for 10 minutes and flake. Melt the butter and add the flour, stirring until smooth. Add the milk and seasonings and cook to medium thickness. Add the fish and the egg yolks and fold in the egg whites. Edge a buttered casserole with the mashed potatoes and add the fish mixture. Sprinkle the crumbs and cheese on top. Bake at 375° for 25 to 30 minutes. Serves 4.

Sauces

I cannot emphasize too much the importance of sauces. For the slight bit of extra work, a sauce served with or on fish will change a plain, ordinary dish of fish into something so appetizing and attractive that it will be classed as gourmet food.

It is also terribly important to interchange the sauces and flavors, and the fun of experimenting will lead to some delightfully surprising combinations and enhance the enjoyment of fish.

ANCHOVY TOMATO SAUCE

½ onion, diced
2 tablespoons olive oil
1 8-ounce can tomato sauce
½ teaspoon orégano
1 2-ounce can anchovies

Brown the onion in the oil. Add the rest of the ingredients and simmer for 5 minutes. This is a wonderful sauce to marinate fish in and then grill! Or pour it over porgies, bass, or blowfish. Makes almost 1 cup.

ALMOND SAUCE

½ cup blanched, skinned, and slivered almonds
3 tablespoons butter
½ teaspoon salt
2 tablespoons lemon juice

Cook the almonds in the butter until golden tan. Add the salt and lemon juice. Pour over broiled or baked fish. This sauce really adds a wonderful touch to any fish. Makes about ¾ cup.

BROILING SAUCE

4 tablespoons butter
1 tablespoon lemon juice
½ teaspoon fish seasoning
¼ teaspoon seasoned salt
2 tablespoons mashed blue cheese
¼ teaspoon Worcestershire sauce
dash of Tabasco sauce
2 tablespoons salad dressing

Melt the butter in a saucepan and add all the other ingredients, mixing well. Pour over fish for broiling, or marinate fish and fry or grill, or serve with the cooked fish at the table. Also terribly good for dipping steamed clams! Makes almost 1 cup.

BARBECUE SAUCE

½ onion, minced
1 cup salad dressing
2 tablespoons catsup
2 tablespoons brown sugar
1 teaspoon Worcestershire sauce
1 teaspoon mustard

Mix everything together and marinate the fish and use for basting. Makes about 1¼ cups.

BEET SAUCE

1 cup mayonnaise
½ cup pickled beets, chopped fine
1 tablespoon chili sauce
1 tablespoon pickle relish

Blend all together. Chill. Wonderful with almost anything, but especially fine with broiled fillet of flounder. Makes about 1½ cups.

EASY LOBSTER SAUCE

1 10½-ounce can frozen lobster soup
½ 10½-ounce can medium cream
1 tablespoon butter

Blend the lobster soup with the cream until smooth. Add the butter and heat to the boiling point. Makes about 1½ cups.

CUCUMBER SAUCE

½ cup sour cream
½ teaspoon onion salt
2 tablespoons vinegar
dash of Tabasco
1 cucumber, peeled and chopped

Blend all ingredients. Chill. This served with porgy will make it a gourmet dish. Makes about 1 cup.

GRAPE SAUCE

1 cup white seedless grapes
¼ cup butter
½ cup white wine

Simmer everything softly for 8 minutes. Absolutely divine served on broiled fish. Makes 1¾ cups.

HORSERADISH AND SOUR CREAM SAUCE

½ cup sour cream
1 tablespoon prepared horseradish
1 tablespoon catsup
⅛ teaspoon salt

Blend all ingredients and chill. Nice with weakfish. Makes ⅔ cup.

HOT MELTED BUTTER
(A MARVELOUS BROILING SAUCE)

1 cup butter
2 teaspoons Worcestershire sauce
2 teaspoons prepared mustard
2 tablespoons chili sauce
2 drops Tabasco
4 teaspoons lemon juice
2 tablespoons chopped parsley

Melt the butter and add all the ingredients. Heat until bubbly. Makes about 1¼ cups.

LOUIS SAUCE

1 cup mayonnaise
1 teaspoon chopped onion
¼ cup chili sauce
1 tablespoon lemon juice
2 tablespoons chopped parsley
½ cup medium cream

Mix all ingredients well. Chill. Serve on the side; especially good with swordfish, striped bass, and tuna steaks. Makes almost 2 cups.

MUSTARD SAUCE

- 1 cup mayonnaise
- 1 tablespoon vinegar
- 1 teaspoon prepared mustard

Blend. Splendid on crisply fried fish or on the side with sautéed soft-shell crabs. Makes about 1 cup.

PARSLEY AND GARLIC BUTTER SAUCE

- 2 tablespoons chopped parsley
- 2 cloves garlic, crushed
- ½ cup melted butter

Add the chopped parsley and crushed garlic to the melted butter and use this sauce to baste blowfish, kingfish, or any other bland fish. Or pour it over fish that has just been cooked, or use as a dip. Makes about ½ cup.

TARTARE SAUCE

- 1 cup mayonnaise
- 1 teaspoon finely minced onion
- 1 teaspoon finely minced pickle or pickle relish
- 1 tablespoon capers
- 1 tablespoon tarragon vinegar

Mix everything together and chill well. Makes about 1¼ cups. This is the good standby for all broiled and fried fish.

ONION SAUCE

1 10½-ounce can cream of onion soup
½ 10½-ounce can milk
3 tablespoons butter
¼ teaspoon salt
⅛ teaspoon pepper

Smooth everything together and simmer. This will dress up a cod like nobody's business! Or pour this sauce over a fish and bake in a 400° oven for 25 to 30 minutes. Makes 1¾ cups.

MAÎTRE D' SAUCE

3 tablespoons butter
1 teaspoon chopped scallion or onion, or a shallot if you can get it
½ cup white wine
¼ teaspoon salt
⅛ teaspoon pepper
2 tablespoons parsley

Sauté the onion in butter until soft. Add the wine, salt, pepper, and parsley and bring to a boil. To use when broiling fish, first broil fish on one side, then turn and pour this sauce over the fish and finish cooking. This will dress up any old fish. But not too old. Makes ¾ cup.

EBB TIDE

Then suddenly there was a change. The mornings became crisp and cool, the noondays warm and golden and the nights cold. Out came the red flannels and electric blankets, and the little stove that was installed in the spring became useful and comforting. The sky turned blue and the bay bluer while the reeds burned to a gold. The pheasants strode across the road and the wild ducks and the wild geese got in formation. There was a stillness that presaged a glory to come.

The tides came in higher and the weaks and the blues came in big runs and there was news about stripers. The snappers went mad and so did the little scallops in the bay.

We got up earlier in the morning to catch the fish that weren't caught all summer. We ran to the beach to catch the last golden warmth of the sun on the sand. We swam in the ocean before it got too cold. We dashed at low tide to get the clams we hadn't had enough of in the summer. We netted crabs like mad. Catch up, catch up, was the tune that ran through the head, with all the good things that will soon be over for the season.

The beach plums ripened and the jelly making took place. Jars were made ready with all kinds of jellies to take home. The freezer was filled with summer things.

Then suddenly that was all over with and the little cottage was prepared for the winter. All soap and candles and matches were stored. Mouse seeds were planted. The curtains, bedding, and spreads were washed and put away. The floors and walls were washed and scrubbed. The lamps, bric-a-brac, pictures, chairs, and tables were covered with clean paper. Clothes were cleaned and tucked away with moth balls. And the refrigerator was scoured as it never had been before.

Shutters were put up and windows and doors were nailed. The electric plugs were removed and the water drained. Finally and sadly we took a last look around and turned the key in the door—*until next year!*

Index

weakfish, 101
Swordfish:
  Amagansett, 92
  Bridgehampton, 93
  broiled, 91
  Portuguese, 92. *See also*
    Casseroles, Chowders,
    117 *and* Louis sauce

Tartare sauce, 132
Three-mile kingfish, 74
Tomato fillets, Ruth's 38
Trolling, 58, 95, 103, 105
Tuna:
  anchovy, 87
  baked, Middle Grounds,
    110
  broiled, Block Island, 88
  canned, Donne's, 88
  chowder, Atlantic, 122
  Napeaque, 87
  steaks:
    Amagansett, 86
    Montauk, 89. *See
    also* Louis sauce.

See also Casse-
roles, Chowders,
117

Wainscott flounder, 39
Watermill fillets, 40
Weakfish:
  baked, Rose Grove, 100
  barbecued, 98
  broiled, 95
  broiled, Wooley Pond,
    100
  catching, 95–96
  Gin Lane, 98
  Italian baked, 97
  Peconic Bay, 99
  Riverhead, 99
  stuffing, 101
  weight, 95. *See* Horserad-
    ish and cream sauce
Westhampton fish casserole,
  121
West Neck snappers, 66
Wooley Pond broiled weak-
fish, 100